Fast Girl

SUZY FAVOR HAMILTON

DEY ST.

AN IMPRINT OF WILLIAM MORROW *PUBLISHERS*

Fast Girl

A Life Spent Running from Madness

DEY ST.

This is a work of nonfiction. The events and experiences detailed herein are all true and have been faithfully rendered as remembered by the author, to the best of her abilities. Some names, identifying characteristics and circumstances have been changed to protect the privacy and anonymity of the individuals involved.

This book contains advice and information relating to mental health care. It should not be used to replace the advice of a trained mental health professional.

HarperCollins books may be purchased for educational, business, or sales promotional use. For information please e-mail the Special Markets Department at SPsales@harpercollins.com.

A hardcover edition of this book was published in 2015 by Dey Street Books, an imprint of William Morrow Publishers.

FIRST DEY STREET BOOKS PAPERBACK EDITION PUBLISHED 2016.

Designed by Shannon Nicole Plunkett

Library of Congress Cataloging-in-Publication Data has been applied for.

ISBN 978-0-06-234620-9

19 20 ov/lsc 10 9 8 7 6 5

To all those with any form of mental illness, whether diagnosed or not, and anyone whose differences cause them to be misunderstood, with the hope that we are moving toward a time of greater understanding and compassion for all

CONTENTS

Prologue

MANIC

I was shaking, still riding the rush. The appointment I'd just left was in one of the fanciest suites at the Wynn. I loved my new condo at the Trump, looking out over the mesmerizing Vegas Strip with all of its bright lights that never slept, but I wasn't ready to go home. I was on fire. I was a winner. I owned this city. I wanted to go out and play. I knew where I was going. I followed my usual path through the Fashion Show Mall, my stilettos clicking on the polished marble floor. Everything around me seemed to pulse and throb, like the blood in my veins. My body was still glowing with pleasure. I wanted more.

This is way better than winning a race, I thought. *This is better than competing in the Olympics. If only my friends, all my fellow runners, could feel what this is like, they'd get it. Why are they still running races? If I'd only known how amazing this felt, I never would have wasted all that time.*

My old life still waited for me in Wisconsin, but I went home less and less these days. I was Kelly now, one of the most highly sought-after escorts in Las Vegas. Suzy, the former professional athlete, the realtor, the wife, the mom—she had disappeared.

I flashed back to the luxurious penthouse suite where I'd spent the past two hours, all sleek furniture and dim light, the shades drawn against the heat and glare outside. It had been my first appointment with this handsome client, but I'd walked in and given him a kiss straightaway, letting my mouth linger on his, my body pressed against him. I wanted him to feel like I was his mistress, like I'd been aching to see no one but him all day. He seemed a bit surprised by how forward I was, but I could tell by his smile that he was pleased. My strategy had worked.

Coming out of the bathroom, where he'd left twelve hundred dollars in cash waiting for me on the vanity, I paused to let him admire me. I was wearing nothing but my six-inch black Louboutins, a black lace bra, and a G-string.

"Holy shit" was all he could mutter.

I smiled, basking in his praise.

"Could you turn around for me?" he continued. "Your body is so fit. What do you do?"

"I was a gymnast in college," I said, using my favorite lie

because it seemed to match my petite but strong frame. And, I had found, it was always a turn-on for my clients.

My head was already buzzing from the glass of pinot noir I'd sipped in the hotel bar before coming upstairs, and his compliment intensified that warmth. So would the glass of wine resting on the bedside table. I felt incredible, ready to go to work. Confidence, power, these were the forces that propelled me now. I took my client to the bed, showing him that I was the one in charge as I stretched him out on the crisp white sheets. He lay there naked and ready. Making my face stern, I straddled him and grabbed his arms, pinning them back over his head with a force that surprised him, holding them there amid the sliding stacks of pillows.

"Do not move your arms," I said with a sly smirk. "Even when I release you. Don't move until I tell you to."

He liked it. I could tell. He was becoming more and more aroused. Ceding control turned him on, a contrast from his daily life as the CEO of a major corporation.

"You're incredible," he said. "You've got the best body I've ever seen."

I HAD EARNED THE TWELVE hundred dollars for two hours of my time, two hours spent doing something I loved. The crisp bills sat in my Louis Vuitton purse, a bag bought for me by another client. The hundreds were like a secret power source, propelling me forward. The confident clip of my walk on the marble floor of the mall made men look up and stare as I passed. An older gentleman with a thick wave of white hair and a well-tailored dress shirt followed me with his eyes. He could tell I was an escort. I could tell he was rich. I loved the power these men had. The wealthier they were, the more important their jobs, the better. It was good to be desired, and even better to be desired by a successful man, to have him choose me as his favorite and request me the next time he came back to Vegas. I could tell this man had already decided that I would be well worth the money it would cost to take me upstairs to his suite. I liked this, too, this secret language I'd learned to speak with my body in the ten months I'd been coming to Vegas, a language that this man, and many others at this point, could understand.

I thought of my next appointment, later that night. By then I'd be buzzing that much more, a smile beaming from my face, showing off my high cheekbones and telegraphing the fact that I was *fun,* the kind of wild girl who could make your dreams come true, not like your wife. That's what my clients always said to me: "I wish my wife were like you. I wish all women were like you." I had worked to achieve a good body, and I loved the praise and knowing I was likely the best sex they'd ever had.

Now that I'd devoted myself to sex, my need to be unsurpassed in the bedroom had replaced that need on the track. But this was even better, because I'd hated the competition necessary to win a race. Everything about being an escort was enjoyable. Although I cared about being at the top of the escort world, too, I never felt that winning made me better than other women, either the other escorts or the wives back home. I was friendly with many of my fellow escorts. I loved trading tips with them. And, believe it or not, I actually felt sorry for the neglected wives and encouraged my clients to think about buying their wives a vibrator, trying some of the things we did together back home. I was doing something I loved and getting paid for it. Why shouldn't I try to help other people in the process? I paused at the window of the Louis Vuitton store. I had all the money I could ever imagine, and I could do with it whatever I wanted. I felt like I should treat myself. Why not? I deserved to be rewarded for my skills, didn't I? I didn't give a single thought to anyone else—my husband, our family. *I think I'll buy that two-thousand-dollar purse* is what I thought.

I pushed through the doors. The attractive, well-put-together saleswoman looked up and immediately came over to help me.

"I'll take that one," I said, pointing at the purse that had caught my attention in the display.

"I love that purse," she said. "We just got those in last week."

She eyed me up and down, just like the man I'd passed, and I could tell she knew how I earned my living, too, but I didn't care. I could feel her admiring how well my dress fit me, how polished my hair and makeup looked. I took the roll of hundreds from my purse and handed twenty bills to her. She didn't even flinch; she just wrapped my purchase in feathery tissue paper and tucked my new purse into one of the store's fabric bags. I floated out of the store and toward the hotel bar, another step toward the high.

With every visit to Vegas since I'd become Kelly, my appearance changed drastically. I was focused on achieving what I thought was the ideal look for a top escort. I was now the number two most highly sought-after escort in Vegas, with my sights set on becoming number one, and I needed to look the part. Of course, as soon as I'd found out the rankings existed, I'd become fixated on rising as high as I could. The positions were determined by ratings given to escorts by their clients, with those coming from well-known "hobbyists," or men who made a point to visit every top escort in Vegas, carrying the most weight. I asked most of my clients to review me and sometimes even gave them a little extra time for free, ensuring a positive write-up. Naturally my rise up the ranks had been fast. Not fast enough for me, of course.

My extensions had gotten longer and blonder, and now my platinum hair cascaded perfectly over my shoulders. I saw a Vegas doctor for Botox, lifting and smoothing my face. I got face peels in Beverly Hills, too, but wore more makeup than ever, popping in at high-end cosmetic counters for professional consultations before sessions with my clients. The beautiful, long false eyelashes I wore gave me a more seductive look. My well-manicured nails were bright red. My trips to the spray-tan salon made my bare limbs look kissed by the desert sun. The tight dresses I wore kept dropping in size, due to my lack of appetite on days like this, when all I wanted to feed was my high. Today, I wore a clingy bright red dress by my favorite designer, Hervé Léger. It fit me like a second skin.

I didn't want to go back to my old life. Not now. Not ever.

Chapter 1
A FEELING LIKE FLYING

We always played on the nature trails near the Wisconsin River, which flowed right below the house where I grew up in Stevens Point. My friends and I were walking together beneath the overhanging oak trees one fall day, looking for fallen branches to build a fort in the shape of a tepee. This would be a fort for girls *only*, where we could hide out. If the boys came by, they'd need to know the password, which we wouldn't tell them. As we continued our search, I shivered in the cool air and looked toward the train tracks, hoping to spot some more building materials and thinking that if I ran a little bit, the motion might warm me up.

"I'm going to go look for some better wood," I said, and took off.

My friends nodded, and we split up to cover more ground. As soon as I rounded the bend, I began to run. This had been my intention all along. I'm not sure why I lied to my friends. It didn't matter. I was flying.

I gathered speed, my sneakers crunching the dry leaves beneath me as they flew over the uneven path with its divots of dead grass, scattered acorns, and twigs, my steps falling with such certainty, I didn't have to look down. Running faster and faster, I discovered a totally new feeling: a perfect mix of euphoria and peace.

When I ran in gym class, I always landed on my toes, instead of on the balls of my feet, like most runners, and so I often thought of myself as a ballerina when I ran because they were always up on their toes, too. But on this day, even though I was running in the same way as usual, my body felt different. I wasn't running because my gym teacher had told me to. I was running because my body was compelled to, for the sheer pleasure of it. Nature seemed so clear to me, the trees swaying in the breeze above me as I passed through the grove where they grew. My stride was so effortless that I picked up my pace even more, my biggest smile on my face. I forgot why I was in the woods in the first place, forgot everything, and began to run like a galloping horse. I was now the horse and didn't ever want to stop. My arms pumped back and forth, my breath visible in white puffs that gusted out of my mouth into the crisp, cold air. I'd already run about a mile when I remembered that I was supposed to be gathering sticks for our dream fort. Suddenly I was afraid my friends would worry about where I was and what I was doing. I had to get back to them quickly. I also knew that I couldn't tell them that I'd run off pretending to be a horse. I heard them calling my name in the distance. I turned back in their direction, and the horse began to pick up the pace again, to a blazing speed now. This was incredible. *Am I really as fast as I feel?* I had no idea, but I knew that I'd found something new to love.

It was such a relief to discover running. I had a very active imagination that made it nearly impossible to concentrate on reading or school, or even on one project at a time. I could never sit still. I always had to be moving, whether I was skiing, mowing the lawn in summer, shoveling the driveway in winter, or cleaning the entire house and scrubbing all the floors while my parents were at work. Our parents instilled a strong work ethic in all of their children, and I was the model child. I always wanted to make my mom and dad happy, like many children do, so I put my need to move into doing things that would please them. But I found as I grew older that constant movement kept my mind empty and at peace, too. If I was still, anxiety and self-doubt crept into my head. I could only stop the motion when I had completely exhausted myself.

Running made me feel better than any other movement, and it seemed I was good at it. I come from a very active and athletic family, but my father was especially gifted. A ski jumper and pole-vaulter in high school, he loved to tell us kids how he'd tried to vault over the fence surrounding his school, only to get his leg caught on the barbed wire. Having grown up poor in rural Wisconsin in a home made chaotic by his alcoholic father, my dad joined the navy as a way out. As an enlisted sailor, he took up boxing, eventually competing in the navy's Golden Gloves amateur boxing competition.

It seemed like he was always jumping over—or off— something; his only fear was of jumping out of an airplane, which he vowed never to do. After leaving the service, he went to college, where he met my mom. When they were first married, my parents were so poor that they lived in a trailer and could only afford tuition for one of them. My dad decided they should flip for it to see who would stay in school. Heads, my mom would stay in nursing school and become a nurse. Tails, my dad would continue studying industrial design and become a graphic designer. The outcome was tails, and so my mom prepared to drop out. However, one of her professors was so impressed with her natural abilities as a nurse that she offered to loan my mom her tuition money so she could pursue her dream. My mom had a long career as a nurse, drawing on her natural nurturing tendencies, which were also evident in the way she raised us four children: my big brother Dan, who was six years older than me, my sister Carrie, who was one year younger than him, my sister Kris, who was three years younger than Carrie, and finally the baby, me.

My sister Kris was my best friend. Although she was only a year older than me, she loved to mother me. We were inseparable for most of my childhood. Because Carrie was quite a bit older than us, closer in age to Dan, she mostly hung out with him, except for when our parents asked her to babysit Kris and me.

When we were growing up, my dad was always the fun guy, so fit that he didn't have a lick of fat on him, who went out for all kinds of behavior most people would consider risky. I had inherited my inability to sit still from my dad; he was always go-go-go. My brother Dan and I were always right there with him, pushing ourselves to keep up. I also shared a love of making art with my dad and Dan, and I enjoyed the fact that this was a common passion that brought me great joy and peace of mind, not anxiety.

Dad's energy and daring often made for an unusual, even remarkable childhood. He had a saying he repeated often, which became our family motto: *Life is a daring adventure or nothing at all.* And we had a poster in our house emblazoned with these words. He was the dad who scrambled up to the highest branch of an oak tree to hang a swing for us. He was the guy firing up his snow blower at ten o'clock at night in a snowstorm, insisting that all of us kids come out and help him. And because he had so much energy, he'd stay outside late into the night clearing our neighbors' driveways, too. I always felt lucky that my home life was so different from my friends'; they mostly just sat around watching TV with their parents. Not us. My dad liked to get out in the snow as much as we kids did. There was a toboggan run with rental sleds right near our house, and we didn't even have to convince Dad to take us. It was his idea. He volunteered to build us snow forts, too, tunneling into the huge mounds of snow in our yard until he had cleared out chambers big enough to hold me and Kris and all of our friends. He used to build the walls so thick that I was scared they would come crashing down on us, but I never admitted my fear to my dad. I wanted him to think I was as brave and strong as he was.

Dad was friendly and talkative, always full of stories and a desire to help people. He often did odd jobs and repairs around the neighborhood. He seemed to be good at everything he tried, and his strength and competence meant that I felt protected when I was with him. But he also liked to push the limits to the extreme, and a part of me was frightened during our adventures together. My father had a great love of sailing, and we often took our sailboat out on the weekends to Lake DuBay, a small lake in central Wisconsin. I was not a big fan of all of the preparation required, so I usually played on the shore while he worked on the boat, sinking my feet into the sand or splashing in the waves. When we did go out together, I never really paid much attention to the actual sailing part, preferring instead to jump into the lake and enjoy a swim while trying to avoid the dreadful seaweed that my imagination transformed into long nightmarish tendrils that could twist around my body and pull me under.

One day I clambered onto the boat with my father, his best friend, and the man's son. My father's friend wasn't any more experienced a sailor than I was. The trip began smoothly enough, even though the lake was strangely deserted for a summer day.

We loaded our supplies, and then my father took control and motioned to me.

"Sit over there, Suzy," he said.

I did as I was told, used to being instructed on where to be and when to duck my head so I didn't get knocked into the water by the boom. As we passed tall pines on our way out of the bay, the skies began to turn gray and the whitecaps started building. The water was even rougher ahead. The gray sky was changing to black, and the wind had become so strong that when we hit the open water, the boat took off like a cannon blast. I had to grab onto a rope and brace myself to avoid falling over.

"Tighten your jackets!" my dad yelled through the gusting wind.

He was the only one without a life jacket, but there was a flotation cushion by his feet, which I kept an eye on as I tightened my own vest until I almost couldn't breathe. I saw fear in my father's eyes, something I had rarely seen before, but he had decided we were going to go sailing, and so, sailing we would go. Once my father had something in mind, there was no stopping him. My dad's sense of determination lasted for a few minutes, and then, with the boat bucking beneath us, even Dad had to admit that this was no day to be out on the open water.

"We need to come about," he yelled, meaning we needed to reverse the boat in order to escape the storm that was about to engulf us and quite possibly tip us over.

I'd experienced what it was like to go under once before, when my father had given my brother control of the boat's rudder. Dan had made a sudden sharp turn, and the boat had flipped. The next thing I knew, I was submerged in the water with the sail pushing my body down. I panicked and fought with the fabric, trying to release myself, but it was wet and heavy, and it wouldn't let me go. At that moment, I remembered my father telling me to always swim down—without panicking—if something like this should happen, as it was the only way to free yourself from the sail. I was determined to survive and found myself kicking my legs hard, until I was clear of the canvas. As my lungs burned, I finally spotted the light of the sky above me. When I popped up, I took the biggest breath I could. I wanted to see my dad because he was my protector. And there he was, pulling me back aboard our boat with his strong arms. Despite the happy ending, the experience scared me, and now here I was, in trouble, on the same lake that had once nearly taken my life.

The waves were coming in over the side of the boat now, the sails whipping around us, as my father struggled to turn us back toward the bay. And then, just like that, my father was gone. I looked back and saw him bobbing in the water, the angry waves covering his head. He was an extremely experienced swimmer, but the fury of the water was unstoppable on this day. My father was in danger. I noticed the flotation cushion was still near me in the boat, but I sat paralyzed with fear until we were too far away for me to reach him anyway. *Why didn't I throw it to him?* I berated myself.

As the boat sailed itself toward the shore, my father became smaller and smaller in the distance. He seemed to be trying to swim to the nearest shoreline, but that was a half mile away, and he would have to swim directly into the wind and waves. Neither his friend nor I had any idea how to turn the boat around to rescue him. Terror and helplessness gripped me. I knew my father was going to drown, and I could do nothing to help him. I could barely see his head bobbing out on the lake. *Had he already drowned?* Panic engulfed me like iron claws. Then I saw a motorboat racing toward where I had last seen him. I prayed they would get to him in time. Just when it seemed that my father was gone forever, the boat reached him. An enormous sense of relief washed over me as I watched them pull him up and out of the water, saving his life. My protector was safe.

My father's friend managed to regain some control of our boat until the speedboat that had rescued my father pulled alongside us. Even in his weakened state, Dad was able to scramble on board. With tears in my eyes, I watched him struggle to lower the sails and finally slow us down enough to ease us back to land. I could see how much the experience had shaken him up, but it did nothing to mellow him. My dad couldn't stop either.

Dan, unlike me, had no trouble keeping up with my dad. We lived near a small ski hill, where my dad was a member of the ski patrol, and we skied every weekend during the winter. I loved to ski, but I was nowhere as talented as my father, who still had the confidence of the youthful ski jumper he had been, and soared down every slope with ease. Dan was really good on the slopes, so good that he was soon racing competitively. It was easy to tell from the look of pure joy on his face that he loved the speed and the adrenaline rush of skiing. In order to emulate both of them, I found myself on the expert hills during our family ski trip to Colorado. Only, I was not a daredevil like them, and I didn't have their skill set, either. In way over my head, I was so terrified to go down the steep slope that I had to slowly slide sideways down the hill on my butt. The moguls became my safety nets, because each one held me for the time I needed to catch my breath and gather the courage to slide down a little farther toward the welcome flat ground below.

I didn't have the same daring personality as Dan, either. As much as I thought I wanted to be like him, and shared his love of art, I didn't chase the rush of dangerous activities the way he did. The older he got, the more erratic his behavior became and the more difficult it became to admire him, much less emulate him. He was quite serious about his high school girlfriend, and when she died of a rare condition called Reye's syndrome, he was devastated. He went to Minneapolis to look for her, even though he'd been told she was gone. He couldn't let her go and truly believed he could bring her back. Her death became a turning point for Dan. As his grief intensified, his mood swings and aggressive behavior worsened, and he was finally diagnosed with bipolar disorder and given shock treatment and lithium. After the treatment, it was as if his true self had been lost, and Dan was never the same again. When my dad lived on the edge, he always clung to some level of control over the situation and himself. I knew my dad would protect me. But now with Dan, it became hard to know if he would stop before hurting himself—or me.

Dan was no different behind the wheel. He once took a curve on his motorcycle so fast that he nearly killed himself in the crash. On the rare occasion I went somewhere with him in his beat-up blue car, he always tore down the highway, REO Speedwagon blaring, the windows down, causing my blond hair to whip around my face. The excitement built as we approached whatever adventure he had planned for the day, just like it always did with our dad, but with an added edge of fear. I wanted to believe he wouldn't risk my life with his, but I wasn't sure. I often wondered if he had no thought of dying at all. When he jumped out of an airplane in his early twenties, I swore I would never, ever do anything like that. But that was only the tip of the iceberg for Dan.

Dan teased me, too, much more than the average big brother harassing the pesky little sister. It wasn't so much any one thing he said or did; it was the intensity with which he pursued me. He pushed and pushed, constantly, trying to make me as upset as possible. I was sensitive, so it didn't take much. And Dan gave more than enough. For some reason, he never targeted my sisters in the same way. Maybe because he saw Carrie as an ally, and besides, as soon as she started dating her boyfriend in high school, she was never around. And Kris didn't challenge him in the same the way I did. It wasn't that I wanted to make him mad. It was just that I couldn't understand why he had to be so loud all the time. He loved Queen, especially the band's songs "Don't Stop Mc Now" and "Bohemian Rhapsody," and when our parents weren't home, he cranked them loudly on the stereo in the living room, listening to them again and again and again, until finally I couldn't take it anymore. I strode into the living room, all righteous indignation.

"Can you please turn it down?" I shouted over the music.

Dan stared at me with a wicked gleam in his eye and turned the music up. Tears started to press against the back of my eyes.

"Please, Dan," I said, my voice shaky. "Turn it down."

He turned the stereo up as loud as it would go. The noise pressed on me, as did his gaze, which was challenging and mean, all trace gone of the big brother who'd once filled my kiddy pool with hot water so I could swim on a cold spring day. Finally, I couldn't fight back my tears anymore, and they poured free. Dan just glared at me. Now, I understand it was Dan's illness that made him behave in this way. But, at the time, I couldn't take his meanness anymore, and I ran to the phone to call my mom. Of course, having me tattle on him only made Dan more determined to show me that he couldn't be controlled. In the summer, he chased me around my grandparents' yard with a snake, waving it wildly in front of me while I ran around screaming. In the fall, the giant dead sunflowers in my grandparents' yard had cracked black centers that looked like burnt-out eyes, and when he came after me with one of those, that was enough to make me cry and beg him to stop, too. But nothing I, or my parents, did or said seemed to have any affect on him. He only harassed me more.

In the mid-seventies, Burger King had these television commercials with this silly little jingle, "Have It Your Way," which Dan turned into its own form of psychological torture.

We were both home alone after school, Mom and Dad still at work. I was in the kitchen looking for a Twinkie to eat. Dan rushed in and slid across the linoleum, always in motion, just like our dad, just like me. He hulked over me, pinning me against the cabinets.

"Have it your way, Suzy," he crooned at me, singing into an

imaginary microphone. "Have it your way. Have it your way at Burger King."

"Dan, stop it," I said.

"Hold the pickle, hold the lettuce, special orders don't upset us," he continued, completely ignoring my pleas.

"Dan, I mean it," I said, my bottom lip trembling as the tears rushed forward. I cried easily and often as a kid, which only gave Dan that much more pleasure. Maybe it was because I was the baby of the family, and Dan was so much bigger and older than me, but I felt like I had no choice but to get my parents involved. And because they always took my side against my brother, I came to expect and need their protection.

He slid back just enough to let me pass, but as soon as I crossed into the dining room, he was right there behind me, singing the stupid jingle over and over again, following me from room to room.

"I'm calling Mom," I cried.

"Have it your way," he sang, totally immune to my tears and threats.

There was nothing I could say or do. Dan was on a tape loop, animated and totally amused. By the time I reached my mom on the phone at the hospital where she worked as a nurse, I was bawling so hard I could barely choke out words. She felt terrible, but there was nothing she could do. She was at work, yes, but there was no stopping Dan when he was like this. And he was like this more and more by the day, even with his medication.

My dad always expected Dan to be able to maintain the

same degree of control over himself that Dad did, and he became furious when Dan could not.

One night, my dad came home already on edge, because it was one of those nights when I'd called my mom at work about Dan, and she hadn't been able to get him to stop doing whatever it was he had been doing. All six of us were at the table, and Dan's behavior set my dad off.

"Dan, stop it," Dad said. "We're trying to have a nice dinner here."

As usual, Dan could never stop once he got started, and he kept carrying on.

"Dan, go to your room," Dad said.

Dan did not get up or curtail his behavior. My father grabbed his plate from the table and threw it against the wall, away from where we were all seated. It shattered, the broken pieces making tiny holes in the wallpaper. Still fit and fast, Dad then grabbed Dan and pulled him the four feet across the floor to his room, forcing him inside and slamming the door. The rest of us sat in silence, our heads down, our food untouched. This was so unlike my dad, who was high energy, yes, but maintained the orderly discipline of the navy throughout his whole life, assigning us kids to specific seats at the table and giving us a particular order in which we had to get ready every morning in the one bathroom we all shared, limiting us all to three-minute showers. I had seen Dad and Dan fight before, but this was too much. I began to cry, and as we sat in silence, the only sound was my snuffling.

Dan started to self-medicate, the way so many mentally ill

people do. One day, when I was twelve and Dan was eighteen, I came home from grocery shopping with my mom to find him passed out on the floor, clutching an empty vodka bottle. Instantly, I could feel Mom's panic rising. This was the first time I'd seen him like this, but I knew it wasn't the first time something like this had happened. Having his bipolar disorder identified hadn't done anything to lessen his desire to obliterate his dark thoughts, and we all worried he was drinking way too much, often to the point of becoming argumentative and reckless, especially when our dad attempted to discipline him, hoping it would help Dan pull it together. My brother had moved down into the basement by now, and another time, our cousin and my dad found him in his bedroom, an empty vodka bottle nearby, pointing one of the shotguns he and Dad used to hunt geese at his head. He didn't respond when our cousin called his name, so Dad rushed in and grabbed the gun out of his hands. Although no one in my family ever mentioned these scenes after the fact, it was impossible to deny the anguish they caused, and a shadow began to creep over our house. I could sense the great tension, even as the youngest, and I began to feel very alone. My oldest sister was close enough to Dan's age that she wasn't home much, and when she was they had an easy camaraderie left over from the childhood years they'd shared as the family's only two children, despite Dan's manic behavior. And although Kris was only a year older than me, and we remained close, she too began to find ways to be out of the house as much as possible.

To me, ours was a family of secret pain. We didn't talk about the moments of fear we felt when Dan went too far, or when my father exploded into a rage. My mother just kept doing what nurses do—care for the hurting people without ever healing them. And I, doted upon as I was, still bore the brunt of Dan's behavior. Nothing was normal, though we pretended it was. I wanted to make up for all of the pain my brother caused. I was going to be perfect.

Chapter 2
PERFECT

When I discovered running, I loved that it was so pure, just my body and me. I was in charge of the outcome, no one else. I didn't have to worry about letting my teammates down like I'd done when I tried basketball, where my legs were too fast for my limited coordination. Or in gymnastics, where my body just wouldn't bend like the other girls', and I couldn't seem to keep up.

Every year, we had an elementary school track meet that included all of the schools in the region. I was running the 400-meter race when I had probably the best running moment of my entire life. As on that day in the woods, I found myself running effortlessly, faster with each stride. As I rounded the final corner in our school's 400-meter track, I found myself leading the pack of young runners by at least seventy-five meters.

The bleachers were crammed with kids from nearby schools, and with the last hundred meters to go, I passed the section of the stands where my schoolmates were seated together. When they realized that I was winning, and by such a big lead, they went wild. "Suzy! Suzy! Suzy!" they chanted as I ran by them.

Soon, all of the students in the stands joined in. A feeling of pride and joy swelled up inside of me. I crossed the finish line, feeling the triumphant sensation of the tape hitting my chest, far before anybody else on the cinder track. As I slowed to a stop, I looked up at the stands, where everyone was beaming down at me, shouting and clapping. *Oh my gosh, all of these people are cheering me on.* In an instant, my triumph turned to self-consciousness. *They're all staring at me.*

I'd found my thing, what I was meant to do. I ran as much as I could after that, not just in school, but on my own, too. Now, my need for perpetual motion was met not as much by frenzied cleaning of our house for my mom, or hours of active absorption in an art project, but by going for a run.

When I joined our middle school's track squad in seventh grade, I was introduced to the concept of training. Everything changed. I was so much faster than the other girls that our coach had me run with the boys' team, so I'd have a more challenging workout. This only went so far, as I was already faster than most of the boys, too. I didn't like being singled out like this, and track practice became anxiety inducing. While I still loved to run, I now found myself unsure about continuing. I'd always tried hard to keep up with my dad and brother, but this was different. Competing against my peers was more complicated. I wanted to win, but I could also tell that my talent made me different. Being different means you are treated differently. I hated not being able to blend in. Thankfully, my sister Kris was already on the track team, and while she wasn't as fast as me—or as obsessed with winning—she was also a gifted runner. We were still very close, and she helped to make practice fun. We would goof around with our teammates, playing pranks on each other and pulling down each other's track shorts, which always made us laugh so much.

My parents were immediately very supportive of my running. They attended all my meets, no matter where they were. My dad borrowed a van from his company and drove my team across the country to meets in other states. The praise and accolades that came with track made my parents proud. I saw that I could distract them from their stress and fears about Dan. But their attention made me feel more pressure to win; there was no way I could let them down, not when I was making them so happy. Kris was generous enough to make sacrifices for me, but I never thought of doing so for her because I couldn't focus on anything but crossing the finish line first. During one cross-country race we ran together, my glasses fogged up, impeding my visibility and slowing my pace. Kris stayed by my side, leading me through the course, until the last two hundred meters. With the finish line just ahead, I lost sight of sisterly solidarity and sped ahead of her, winning the race. At the time, I thought nothing of such behavior. As long as I won, nothing else mattered. Of course, looking back, I can see how selfless her act was.

I was completely focused on my running, and how it made me feel. Running was my answer to everything. The more tension-filled the situation with Dan became at home, the harder I trained. The harder I trained, the more I won, and the more I was taken away from home by practice and meets, which also took me away from the family drama. Unfortunately, this didn't bring me any relief, though. My anxiety and the added drive it caused within me led me to pull up into myself. This became the pattern of my life, and it fit. We didn't share our emotions in my family anyway, and by training constantly and pushing myself on the track, I could deny I had any. As I got older, I became even more focused, and winning became even more complicated. In my freshman year at Stevens Point Area Senior High, I won every race, and all of the local and regional races too. Then, at the statewide meet, I won for the mile, and in cross-country for the two-mile, or 3,200-meter, race. My parents, and my hometown, were overjoyed, but I became instantly miserable.

Sure, I wanted to win. I liked to win. But, in truth, I *needed* to win. Even as I stood with my teammates, receiving my medal, the wheels in my head were turning. *Now I have to win every state meet I ever run. There's no choice. If I were to lose, I'd let everyone down—my parents, my coach, my community—and that can't happen.*

And thus began a cruel cycle in my life. The more obsessed I became, the faster I ran; the faster I ran, the more notoriety I received; and the more notoriety I received, the more obsessed I became. Soon, even winning wasn't enough.

AT THE END OF MY sophomore year, the '84 Summer Olympics were held in Los Angeles. From the moment I started running competitively, the Olympics were in my sights. Becoming an Olympian now became my obsession.

I'd just won the 1,500 meters in a record time of 4:19 at the U.S. Junior Nationals. That year, the Junior Nationals were held in conjunction with the Olympic trials in order to give us student athletes a feel for international competition. International competition meant larger crowds, more intense scrutiny, and that I'd be running alongside Olympians.

Before my race, my coach brought me to the warm-up track where the Olympic runners were all stretching. I stood beside him, watching uncertainly.

"Okay, Suzy, go warm up," he said, nodding toward the runners.

I froze. These were the great Olympians I'd always idolized. Who was I to warm up with them?

"I can't go in there," I said, ducking my head in shame.

"Of course you can, Suzy," he said. "You're the Junior National Champion."

I shook off his words and stepped away from the grass near the track. My coach didn't understand. No one could. I knew that I was in constant danger of failing at any moment. I knew that I was never good enough. But my coach was confused and frustrated, though he finally let me warm up where I felt like I really belonged: in the parking lot.

Even so, when I saw the runners I most admired fly around that track, being cheered on by the whole world, I knew I *had* to be an Olympian. I decided I was willing to do anything it took to make this happen. School, relationships, family, anything that didn't directly support that goal would have to be put aside.

For an overwhelming majority of my cross-country races during my junior and senior years, I beat all my competitors by a substantial distance. Given that, I should have been flush with confidence. Instead, meets became a source of dread. My mind began to go to very dark places before each and every race. As the hours before a meet ticked away, my stomach became a fist of nerves, and I had one thought: *If I could just break my leg, I wouldn't have to run this race.*

I wasn't alone in these feelings. In 1986, during my senior year in high school, one of the top college runners in the country, twenty-one-year-old junior Kathy Ormsby, was running the 10,000-meter race in the National Collegiate Athletic Association's outdoor track-and-field championships when she found herself in fourth place. She suddenly veered off the track and jumped from a bridge in a suicide attempt that left her paralyzed. This was obviously big news in the running world, shocking many. I was too young and, frankly, too consumed to see the connection between Kathy and myself. I just kept my head down and trained harder, convinced I would never let myself fall to fourth place in any race.

I took it upon myself to do extra miles in the morning before school, but that quickly proved too difficult, as it meant waking up at 6 A.M. to run, doing a full school day, and then training with my team afterward. So I began running at lunch during the week, usually after eating only an apple, while my friends in the cafeteria flirted with boys and planned the next party or night of drinking and hanging out. Kris didn't feel compelled to put in extra training, and so we didn't spend as much time together as we once had. My dad began asking if he could run with me, but the idea of having him get involved with my training so directly felt like more added pressure, so I didn't let him. Instead I sought his praise in other ways, continuing to take on extra chores around the house, such as the laundry and ironing, and mastering skills I knew my dad admired. I already loved art, so it was easy for me to throw myself into art projects at school, in hopes he'd appreciate my work. He built stilts for us kids to use, and I was the one who used them the most. I was also the one who mastered the unicycle he brought home, sometimes riding it to school. My family didn't have to be on my runs with me to see how hard I was pushing myself. Eventually my mother stopped me in our kitchen, with concern in her eyes.

"Just take a day off," she said.

Not an option, I thought as I shrugged and went out for a ten-mile run. As I ran, my worries ricocheted through my head: *I'm not fast enough. I'm not thin enough. My body has to be stronger and tighter. I can't let anyone beat me because I'll let my family down. I'll let my coach down. I'll let my community down.*

ONE NIGHT IN HIGH SCHOOL, I was babysitting for a single mom who lived nearly two miles from me. She was friends with my older sister Carrie, and the two of them were out together that night. The baby was little, and soon after I arrived he fell asleep.

The mother had assured me that she would be home by ten, which was important to me because I had a big regional race the next day. My dad was the meet promoter, and the event was a huge deal in our small community of twenty-eight thousand people. It was my hometown. My dad was hosting the race. I had to win. Around nine thirty, I stretched out on the couch. The next time I looked at my watch it was ten thirty, and the woman wasn't home yet. My brain went to the dark place. *Why aren't you here? I'm going to lose tomorrow because you said you would be home at ten, and I'm not going to be able to get my sleep, and I'm going to lose. My father will be mortified. My whole town will be angry.* I forced my eyes shut. I felt guilty, because I knew I shouldn't go to sleep when I was supposed to be caring for a child. But I needed my rest for my race in the morning. I must have finally drifted into sleep. Somehow, while I was sleeping, I got off the couch, went to the door, and opened it; I had a very clear vision of my hand on the knob.

The next thing I knew, I was running. It was like I woke up, and my legs were already flying beneath me. The night was dark and hazy, with the shadows from the streetlamps suddenly coming up on me, then falling away behind me, as I ran faster and faster. I felt like I was sprinting through a nightmare. I was washed in waves of panic, but I couldn't stop my legs. They were moving of their own will. *Oh my god, what did I just do? I left that baby all alone.*

I wanted to stop. I wanted to turn back. All I could do was run. By this time, I was about half a mile from my house and nearly hysterical. I ran in the door and burst into my parents' bedroom. I leaned down over my mom, in tears, and woke her up.

"Mom, I left the baby," I said, crying hard.

She sat up, surprised.

By this point, my mom and dad were both fully awake. My dad got dressed and led me to the kitchen. He told me to get into his car so he could drive me back to the woman's house. I was petrified that we'd discover that something terrible had happened to the baby. As soon as we parked, I raced into the house, my dad close behind me. I opened the door as gently as I possibly could, my hand shaking, and peeked in: the baby was asleep in his crib, just as I'd left him earlier in the night. My dad then left me sitting on the couch, placing a book and a glass of water near me. The baby was safe, but I couldn't calm down. I felt terrible about what I'd done, and my heart was pounding. When the mother came home a few moments later, she was concerned when I confessed to what had happened, but relieved that her son was safe. Needless to say, that was the end of my babysitting for a while.

Finally, I made it home and climbed into bed. I got up the next day, and I won the race.

Feeling out of control, I found one thing I did have power over: what I ate, or more accurately, how little I ate. If my parents pushed, I ate even less. Between the minuscule amount of food I was eating and the excessive training, my body was starving itself. But I didn't think about that. I was running faster by eating less. I liked the results.

At this point, my biggest goal was to get into a college with a great running program. The college-level runners I saw were far thinner than I was. They all looked anorexic, and I wanted that for myself. I tried to starve myself completely, but with all my training it just wasn't sustainable, so I became bulimic instead. I worked out a complicated system, where I binged on a whole tray of brownies or a bunch of pasta—I think my body craved sugar—and then I purged. Right afterward, I felt awful, worse than before I had stuffed myself. It was a vicious, terrible cycle, and one that I hid completely. I'm sure my parents suspected, but if they had ever confronted me I would have become furious. My parents stayed silent, true to the culture of our family. They never wanted to do anything that might upset me—the one in the family who made them the most proud.

I became friends during this time with a fellow runner from Colorado. We had met at several national meets, and somehow we realized that we shared a secret. We confided in each other at meets and in the letters we exchanged about bingeing and purging. But she was the only one who knew, or at least the only person who acknowledged my behavior. Our friendship was incredibly reassuring for me because it made me feel like what I was doing was safe, good for me even. She was a great runner, and she threw up after she ate, so clearly there was nothing wrong with me doing it. It became our bond, a bond in sickness and obsession.

While I was considering colleges, I originally dreamed of going to school in California. I wanted to live a life completely different than the one I'd always known in Wisconsin, where I could train under the palm trees and spend weekends at the beach. Stanford was among the many schools to recruit me because of my national standing as a runner, but my top choice was UCLA. My parents didn't really understand what it would mean for me to attend a prestigious school like Stanford, and my dad suggested I go to a small school in Stevens Point, so I could be close to home. I knew I could never compete at the level I dreamed of unless I went to a school with a top track program. But when I began the application process, it became clear that my poor grades would make it difficult for me to get into many of the schools, even with my gift for running. I barely squeaked into UCLA, but as much as they wanted me for their running program, they made it clear that it wasn't going to be easy for me to maintain my place there.

And then I met with Peter Tegen, who coached the women's running team at the University of Wisconsin. Originally from East Germany, he had an aura of greatness about him, and he was known as one of the best coaches in the country. The university had a summer running camp for the best high school runners in the state, which I had attended, so I had met Peter and he had seen me run. My sister Kris was a freshman at the university and on the running team, so I continued to see Peter at her events. When I visited on my recruiting trip, it was clear that all the runners on his team had a huge amount of respect for him. During the practice I sat in on, I watched with interest as Peter walked into the room and the entire team immediately stopped talking or goofing around. As he spoke, they hung on his every word. I was so impressed with him and what seemed like his drive to get his athletes to succeed. I even liked that he didn't recruit me as aggressively as other programs. It just wasn't in his nature to be pushy or flamboyant, and this made me even more convinced that his priorities were in the right place and that he was the ideal coach for me. The University of Wisconsin had just won the national championships in cross-country, so becoming part of the best running program in the country was also very enticing. How could I not attend the university in my home state, which was so proud of me and had done so much to support my running? Peter also told me during my recruiting trip that another Wisconsin runner I'd also become friends with during state meets, Mary Hartzheim, was attending Wisconsin on a full scholarship, and that clinched the deal for me. "Where do I sign?" I asked, in my mind already decorating the dorm room I would share with Mary.

I, too, was granted a full scholarship to the university. Madison was two hours from Stevens Point, so I could still visit home often, while enjoying the kind of freedom most kids crave when they go off to college.

By choosing my family and running for Wisconsin over UCLA, I focused all of my attention on the two things that mattered to me the most without realizing how much I was limiting my horizons. Wisconsin in the 1980s still maintained much of the small-town innocence and charm of the '50s. No one locked their doors and everybody looked out for each other. Most people focused on their family, their church, and their hometown pride, which was why college and even high school athletics were followed with such fervor. There wasn't much else to get excited about.

There was still a stigma at this time about people who were mentally ill; in fact, the term we used was *crazy*, and crazy people belonged in a loony bin. I'm not proud of it, but I sometimes felt that way about Dan. When my parents asked me if I wanted to go see a psychiatrist, probably to discuss my food issues and maybe how Dan's illness was affecting me, I was appalled.

"Absolutely not," I said. "I will never go to a psychiatrist."

When I was growing up, in the 1970s, mental illness was rarely discussed. Remember, we were not too many years away from the time when mentally ill patients were shuttered away, sent to live in asylums forever, separated from and even forgotten by their families. Some were subjected to horrific treatments like lobotomies, which today seem barbaric, the stuff of horror films. And while that practice had fallen out of favor by the time I came of age, there remained a horrible stigma attached to being mentally ill. It wasn't just my family who avoided this topic. There was fear, of course, but also a lack of knowledge about the kinds of mental illness that exist, their symptoms, and the courses of action that might be taken by parents, school systems, and government. Today depression, anxiety, and bipolar disorder are as commonly discussed as other ailments like diabetes and cancer. Everyone knows that these conditions exist, and most everyone knows there is treatment available.

With all the knowledge and experience I have now, it is plain to me that my brother suffered from mental illness at a very young age. But even after he was diagnosed, we never acknowledged it or discussed it as a family. My parents loved Dan and did what they could to help him, but they just didn't understand him or his illness. It became easier for them to let him fade into the background and focus instead on my sisters and me, and especially my running and the great sense of pride it inspired in them. Perhaps it was just the culture, or perhaps it was our own culture of denial, but I do believe if we'd had the tools, the knowledge, and the bravery to openly face that truth, the history of my family could have been altered. I think that more than mental illness, however, the most serious issue that plagued our family was silence.

Chapter 3
GO BADGERS

Mary and I pretty much commanded the track team from the first practice of our freshman year, and it was no shock how the older team members felt about that. We weren't surprised that the seniors didn't like a couple of freshmen coming in and commanding attention, but we couldn't believe just how catty they were at times. One of the girls even pulled Coach Peter aside to air her grievances.

"They're running too fast," she said.

Obviously, that's not a concern that holds much weight with a track coach. And their complaints only made Mary and me more determined to be the stars of the team. We knew we were talented, and we weren't going to take that kind of attitude from anyone. We got even by running even faster in practice. My devotion to running dovetailed perfectly with the training philosophy of my new coach. He proudly displayed many of the stereotypes of his German background—stoic, disciplined, and tough. Over the years, he had attracted many critics for his cold demeanor and his drive to win. None of that bothered me. He had a favorite saying back then: "I don't produce sissy runners." This made perfect sense as far as I was concerned. What he did produce was the best collegiate female runners, and that was all I needed to know.

Peter was definitely a father figure to all of his girls, but Mary and I saw him as nothing short of God. He trained us to race in the European style, which meant being prepared to take a little abuse, a spike in the shin or an elbow in the ribs, and still keep running as fast as possible. He also trained us to be more aggressive ourselves, a new concept to me. I was a rhythm runner: I did best when I trained to get into peak physical shape, set a pace just at the top of what I could do, and stuck with it for the entire race. So, some of what Peter pushed me to do was outside of my comfort zone, but I also knew that a strategic move or show of aggression could help me in races where I was pitted against a woman who was actually faster.

My first big track race as a college athlete was the indoor mile. I felt like the eyes of the entire state were on me. I was a local, and I had chosen to attend a state school rather than head off to seek glory (and sunshine) in California. While most would have seen this as a tick in the win column out of the gate, of course I didn't. For me it meant I had no choice but to win. As usual. I did exactly what Peter told me to do, always, and I did win that first race. In fact, when I stuck to his plan, I always won. I did have one setback in the fall of my freshman year, when I came in second in my race at the cross-country nationals. I wasn't used to losing, and I didn't like it one bit, but cross-country was not my specialty, so it wasn't the end of the world. Also, the runner who won was Canadian, which meant I was still the best American female runner in that event. I had lost, but as a freshman in college I was already holding my own against the best.

Peter praised the runners who he felt earned that attention, and I came to crave his approval, just as I had with my dad. Determined to make Peter proud, I made sure to never let him down. I was golden, and determined to stay that way. Unsurprisingly, Peter's attention inspired jealousy from some of my teammates. This didn't feel good, but I honestly didn't care. I only cared about what Peter cared about, and Peter cared about winning.

Peter had good intentions, but he was strict, and not just about his training regimen and how he expected us to behave during races. Peter recruited the most driven runners he could find, runners who, like me, were willing to do absolutely *any-thing* to be the best, and many of the girls he trained over the years developed eating disorders. I don't think that there is a direct link, or blame to be placed. The 1980s were a different time in sports, and we were much less sophisticated in our knowledge of nutrition and how it could impact performance. There were no perfectly calibrated dietary guidelines for athletes, no protein shakes or energy bars. We were also teen-age girls, having our first experience away from home. We didn't think about balancing what was on our plates. We'd eat an entire bag of cookies, or whatever junk food was salty, fatty, or sweet, and then do what we had to do to get rid of the excess in our bodies. None of the coaches or trainers thought to address anorexia and bulimia as mental health disorders that required intervention and treatment.

The bulimia I had developed in high school was full blown by the time I started college. I didn't think I could change my behavior around food if I was going to keep winning, and I knew I couldn't stop winning.

So, I devised a method to manage my bulimia. Every day, I brought two bags to the dining hall—one plastic, one paper. I stuffed the plastic bag with large quantities of the kinds of comfort foods that were popular in the Midwest—casseroles, mashed potatoes, and brownies—and then put the plastic bag inside the paper bag, so no one could see what was inside. I then went back to my room at a time when I knew Mary had class, so I'd be alone, and I binged on my stash. Then, I purged right into the plastic bag, still inside the paper bag, and carried it out to the trash can in the hallway. There were plenty of girls who threw up in the bathroom of my dorm so everyone could hear. But I never wanted anyone to know the measures I was taking to stay lean and fast. I needed to main-tain my façade of perfection.

I liked the feeling of control the bulimia gave me. Right after I threw up, I felt physically terrible, worse than I had before I'd eaten all of that garbage. But soon after, I felt clean and orderly, which was a relief compared to how I usually felt. As much as I bent under the will of my father, first, and then Peter to determine what my priorities would be and what I needed to do to achieve them, sometimes I did pine to have my own voice. But that desire was overshadowed by the anxiety that came with my quest to be perfect, all the time, and my fears around growing up, boyfriends and sex, and my family. The bulimia felt like one thing I could control.

No matter how skinny I was, I always felt heavy, especially because I didn't have what I thought of as the perfect running body. I had big boobs, and they were noticeable when I ran. Deeply insecure, I felt it wasn't enough to be a great runner; I had to look like a great runner, too, and I was constantly worried about the fact that I didn't. I did everything to hide my large breasts, specifically ordering a team shirt that was too large for me and then cutting it apart and altering it to hang even more loosely on me. It didn't work. One day my coach called me into his office and read me a letter he'd received from a female supporter of the team: "Tell Suzy it would be a good idea for her to wear two sports bras when she runs."

As these words left his mouth, I slunk lower in my chair, unable to meet his eyes. I was mortified. I couldn't understand why someone had sent this letter. What did this woman know about my body? What business was it of hers how many sports bras I wore? I was trying to be a serious athlete. I devoted nearly every waking moment to my training, and now I had to fight this judgmental voice in my head, too? I slunk out of his office, deeply ashamed. But I started wearing two sports bras when I ran.

My shame turned to rage later in my college track career, when I learned that one of the coaches of the men's track team had filmed me while I was training and showed his team members a video of my breasts bouncing as I ran. A shot putter on the team, who happened to be my friend, told me. The coach was disciplined, but not before I'd been humiliated all over again. What the coach meant as sexist ogling, I took as a testament to what was wrong with me.

Soon after the video incident, I had a stress fracture to my femur, which is extremely hard to do and extremely painful. The injury could become serious, and it meant that I had to back off from my training. This pushed me to obsess about my weight that much more. To make matters worse, my injury wouldn't heal. I gave myself a rest, but I wasn't getting better. Before then, I'd never thought about what bulimia might be doing to my body other than keeping it thin. I wasn't aware of how the lack of nutrients in my body might make me infertile or destroy my bone density. When I got injured, I began to observe other runners on the team and notice that the girls who were obviously anorexic became injured more frequently than those who weren't. But I still wasn't concerned enough to stop my bingeing and purging, which I felt I needed to do more than ever now in order to keep my weight down. It wasn't until later, in a nutrition class, that I gained the kind of specific knowledge that meant I could no longer downplay the connection between eating disorders and injuries.

My health wasn't the only thing that took a backseat to my running in college. When I entered the University of Wisconsin, my academic adviser was well aware of how poor my grades had been in high school and how difficult it had been for me to get into college, even with my obvious running talent. At the start of my freshman year, my classmates were given the opportunity to test out of our required math and English classes. Not only did I not qualify to skip the basic courses in these subjects, but my particularly low scores on the English portion revealed that I most likely had a learning disability. I had such myopic focus on my running that I didn't take the time to really absorb what this might mean, and no one I encountered in the school's administration or athletics department ever addressed my academic prospects: they simply wanted me to keep winning.

By the time of my first meeting with my adviser during freshman year, I was already having trouble with my classes. "I'm really struggling," I said.

"You're going to make it," he said. "I guarantee you. We will get you through college. You will have no problem."

My adviser arranged for me to have a tutor so my grades wouldn't become so low that I was disqualified from competing. Then he pulled out the catalog and helped me schedule a course load of what the other athletes and I called the "blow-off" classes. It didn't matter that college was supposed to prepare me for a future career, after running. I was going to enjoy the treatment of a star athlete, which meant easy classes and professors looking the other way if I didn't do my work on time or well. I was not accountable for anything except how I did on the track. This suited me perfectly. The normal star athlete major was physical education, but I couldn't pass kinesiology, and so I lucked out and got to fall back on a major that was actually something I loved almost as much as running: art. Even so, I still couldn't make it through college on my own. I had a tutor who wrote a couple of my papers for me. I was not her only client, though, and she once wrote the exact same paper for twenty-five student athletes. This incident almost got me expelled, but I knew deep down that I would never get kicked out of school. I was too valuable as a runner for the school to make that move. Another time, I had a psychology final the day after I got back from the national cross-country meet where I'd just placed second. I hadn't studied one bit. I hadn't had time, and even if I had all the time in the world I didn't have the ability to study. I never had and I didn't know how. Mary and I were together in our room when I confessed.

"I'm going to fail," I wailed. "What am I going to do?"

Mary was the kind of person who always pulled everything off at the last minute, with maximum grace, and she knew exactly what I should do.

"Call the professor," she said.

I hated confrontation or drawing attention to myself in any way, and I was extremely nervous, but I gathered my courage. When I got the professor on the phone, I got right to the point.

"I know we have our final tomorrow," I said. "And I didn't study one bit. I just got second at the cross-country nationals."

"Don't worry," he said. "You don't have to take it. We'll just average your grades from your previous tests, a C and a D, and give you a C."

"Thank you," I said.

And that was that.

I was relieved and grateful. Now I could get away with not studying, without a single consequence. Sitting in a classroom was torture for me, and I hated anything I wasn't good at, so I didn't even try. As far as I was concerned, I was already good at something—so why bother with the rest?

Thankfully, I had Mary. She became like a sister to me. She was my best friend, and the only person in my life who ever made me feel like I could completely be myself. Mary was as serious about running as I was, but unlike me, she was incredibly bright and always did very well in school, even when she was putting papers off until the last minute because she was in the midst of some wild adventure.

I was in awe of Mary and so glad to be her friend. She was a total tomboy, but gorgeous even so. She had beautiful wavy brown hair, a huge smile, and a natural glow, so she never had to wear makeup. I used to have fun trying to make her more feminine—curling her hair and making up her face. But even without that, all of the boys had crushes on her, and it was obvious why. She was the life of every party. She didn't need to be the center of attention, she simply was. People paid attention to Mary and wanted to be with her. She had a profound influence on me. Mary wanted to be a standout athlete, too, but she wasn't obsessive like I was. She wasn't plagued by anxiety. She was the one person who made me relax.

We couldn't drink much, because we had to stay in top shape, but there were a few times, just after nationals, when we let loose. These are some of my fondest memories of college. Just before Christmas vacation during freshman year, we got all dolled up. I curled my hair and painted my face, then

Mary let me do the same for her. We bundled up against the cold weather and hurried over to this bar called the Kollege Klub, known as the KK. As we walked up to the door, I took in deep gulps of the cold, damp air. Snow was on the way. I was nervous. I'd never been to a bar before and I was well aware that as freshmen, we looked like babies to the older students. I was afraid, too, of doing anything that might harm the image of perfection that I had worked so hard to create. But I wanted to be wherever Mary was. Plus, we'd been working hard all semester. We had made it through our first set of finals. I felt like we deserved a little fun. As we flung the door open, a gust of warm, beer-soaked air washed over us, along with an Aerosmith guitar lick and the shouts of some excited male students who had clearly been at it a while. A beefy older student in a letterman's jacket stopped us short at the door, and my heart sank. Mary laughed. I looked more closely. He was on the track team, and he knew us, which also meant he knew we were freshmen. He let us in anyway.

I laughed, giddy with excitement and relief, and followed Mary into the bar, where our fellow athletes were already calling out her name and waving her over. As we shed our coats and threw them over the backs of chairs, I already felt at home. It didn't take long for us to learn how to get guys to buy us drinks. Before I knew it, Mary and I were together in the area of the bar that had become an impromptu dance floor at some point in the night, drunk and happy, dancing so hard we called it our second workout of the day. We drank and danced until last call, soaking up every second of this freedom and abandon. Before I was ready, the lights came on, revealing the sticky floor and bleary college students, getting in every dance and flirtation. Only then did we force ourselves out into the winter night. Giggling madly, we fell into a cab together and rode back to our dorm room. In our pajamas, we both climbed into Mary's bed and waited for the night's final treat—a giant pizza from Uncle Jim's, the best pizza on campus. When it was delivered, we ate every bite, breaking one last taboo before passing out in our little bunk beds. Those were the best times, in college, because we were actually living like normal students.

I wish there had been more moments like these. Even if that night off was bad for my running, it was good for my spirit.

Chapter 4
I'M GOING TO
MARRY HIM

In January of my freshman year, a friend who I had gone to high school with set me up on a blind date with one of his baseball teammates. He had also come to the University of Wisconsin, and he wanted to introduce me to a freshman pitcher from California, Mark Hamilton. I found a way to spy on Mark beforehand. I know it was shallow of me, but if I was going to take the time to go on a blind date, I wanted to at least make sure I found the guy attractive. The day I checked him out, Mark was wearing white jeans and a blue shirt, and to me, he looked like Val Kilmer in *Top Gun*, with that same flattop. I thought he was gorgeous.

I went out and bought a cute pink sweater with a lace

collar. I purposely wanted to look very sweet and innocent for the date. Not that it was an act. I hadn't really dated much in college yet and I was still a virgin.

I was actually late for our first date because I was at a doctor's appointment for my injured femur, so I called Mark to let him know. When he eventually came to pick me up, he brought me flowers. *Oh, wow, I just meet this guy, and he's already bringing me flowers. Nobody's ever done that before.*

Mark didn't have a car, so we walked up Bascom Hill, which is the heart of the university, and then on to the restaurant. I was wearing these silly boots that were trendy but slippery. When my feet hit a patch of icy ground and started to fly out from under me, it gave me an excuse to grab him.

"Can I hold on to your arm?" I asked.

It really wasn't like me to be so forward, but from the moment I met Mark, I felt like I knew him. He held out his arm, and I slid mine through his, and we walked the rest of the mile and a half to have pizza. Once we got to the pizzeria, we slid into a booth, grateful for the restaurant's warmth.

We were both too nervous to eat that night, worried about getting food on our faces or spilling sauce on our shirts. But everything else between us was relaxed and the conversation flowed easily. I knew he was at school on a baseball scholarship, and he knew I was a runner, but we didn't talk much about our sports. I was obsessed with Madonna at the time, and my friend had told me that Mark's parents had recently moved near her in Malibu, so I asked him about that. We told each other stories and made each other laugh.

As we walked back to my dorm, my heart was fluttering

with happiness and excitement. We stopped outside and Mark smiled at me.

"I have a baseball trip, but I'll call you in a few days when I'm back," he said.

I smiled up at him. He leaned in and kissed me on the lips. It was just a little kiss, a peck, really. But that was enough for me. *I'm going to marry this guy*, I thought, as I tore up the stairs to my room, so excited to tell Mary every detail about my night. All I could think of was whether or not he was going to call, and when the day of his return came and went without the call, I was so disappointed. I had been so sure about him. And then, the next day, my phone rang.

For our second date, we hung out in his dorm room. After that, I saw him every single day. Mark would later tell me that he'd gone out with me just to be able to say he'd done so, really—I was always in the school paper, and people on campus knew my name. He'd expected me to be just another arrogant athlete who could only talk and think about myself, and he'd been pleasantly surprised by how humble I was, how easy it was to talk to me, and how much fun we had together. I'd never met anyone like Mark. I was used to men from Wisconsin, who were good, strong, hard workers, but reserved to the point of silence. Mark was open-minded and stylish, and he wanted to talk about *everything*. He became my new obsession, second only to my running. Fortunately, because he was an accomplished pitcher, he understood what it took to be an athlete, and he understood that running had to come first for me. In fact, looking back, he was probably glad I had something else to focus on besides him.

I now created a new routine. Every day after classes, I went to track practice, then lifted weights with the rest of the runners. I always did my workout as fast as I could because I couldn't wait to see Mark. I was always the first person out of the weight room and into the showers. I made sure I looked good, and then I hurried to wherever he was. Mark was taking night classes, and had a nutrition class that was taught by video, so there was no instructor in the room. I would literally go to his class and sit next to him while he watched. Mark didn't take blow-off classes like I did. He was an A student, and he got his only B that semester, because of me. I gave him mono, too, but luckily neither of these turned him against me. And it was in Mark's nutrition class that I finally learned the damage my bulimia was doing to my body and began to think about trying to stop my self-destructive behavior. But I couldn't give up my belief that it helped me to win.

Once we started to spend all our time together, Mark's influence began to rub off on me. Although Mark never asked me about my bulimia directly, he did gently urge me to eat when we were together, and he noticed when I'd skip a meal. Eventually, I opened up to him. Mark was concerned. I was, too, after my fractured femur had taken so long to heal. With Mark's support, I stopped purging and adopted a more balanced diet. He also called me out when he met up with me at a party one night and found me wasted, having indulged in one of my very occasional nights of binge drinking. As he pointed out, it wasn't good for me on any level, especially as I was so well known on campus.

Mark also helped me to address one of my greatest fears:

sex. Here I was dating a man I was head over heels for, but I was still terrified of getting pregnant or doing something that might conflict with my image of perfection. Mark gently pushed, and I kept refusing, until finally, on his birthday, I agreed. Since we both had roommates, and because Mark wanted to make my first time special, he booked a hotel room for the night. But when the moment came, my nerves took over, and I couldn't go through with it.

"No," I said. "I'm sorry. I can't."

Of course Mark was kind, and assured me we could wait until I was ready. Well, the next day, we were hanging out alone in his dorm room after class and started making out on his bed.

"Let's have sex," I said.

"Why did you wait until today?" he asked, laughing. "We had this great hotel room, privacy. I wanted to make it special."

I didn't need a hotel room to make it special for me. I knew that sex was the next stage in the relationship, and once it happened I wanted more. But with sex came the fear of pregnancy, and I couldn't risk going on the pill and having my parents find out. I forced Mark to go with me to Planned Parenthood for extra spermicide.

A few months after we'd started sleeping together, Mark convinced me to take a shower with him in his dorm. It didn't take long for word to spread that Mark was in the shower with Suzy Favor. A group of guys busted in and caught us together. I was horrified. Mark threw me a towel. I wrapped myself up completely and hurried back to Mark's room, where I literally climbed into his closet to hide. Mark was close behind me, laughing, but he stopped when he saw how upset I was. He leaned into his closet to talk to me.

"Suzy, it's not a big deal," he said. "Really, it's not."

"I'm going to get kicked out of school. I'm going to lose my scholarship."

"You're not," he said. "Seriously, trust me."

There was nothing he could say to convince me until several weeks passed and nothing came of it. That's how paranoid I was.

Mark was soon taking care of me and seeing to my every need, in the same way that Peter replaced my running shoes whenever I requested—something he didn't do for any of the other runners. And in the same way that my father and mother had always done their best to shelter me from conflict or difficulty, especially my brother's teasing. Whereas I'd once spent all of my time with Mary and my sister Kris, I now constantly hung out with Mark. Mary was extremely independent, and this shift in our friendship didn't make her feel any less close to me. Kris had quit the track team during her sophomore year, and because I'd felt the need to train more than ever, we'd already reached a point where we rarely spent time together, and we were no longer as close as we had once been. Whereas Kris had always been my biggest ally within the family, she began to pull away from me and toward my other siblings, who were also being left out of the winner's circle.

What little connection we'd maintained since she quit the track team began to dissolve over time.

Mark quickly saw how much I was struggling academically and did his best to help me, teaching me study techniques and encouraging me to see tutors. When we were in the library, I couldn't sit still and often goofed around, trying to make him laugh. When we were in his dorm room, I tried to distract him and get him to make out with me. He insisted on studying, no matter what, because he was determined to keep his grades up. When Mark realized I wasn't just being lazy but had a real learning difficulty, he started to help in more direct ways. While he never wrote papers for me, he did often read mine over for me and make corrections. When I took an architecture class the semester after him, I used Mark's old exams to get through. The more I relied on Mark, the more I felt like I couldn't live without him.

At the beginning of our sophomore year, when all of the students returned to campus, I was living in a house off campus with Mary and some of our running teammates. I'd been feeling distant from Mark, who had spent the summer at home in Malibu. When Mark returned in the fall, a friend I'd been spending most of my time with that summer seemed upset by the idea of no longer having me to herself and began putting pressure on me to break up with Mark. So I did. Always a pleaser, I wanted to make her happy, and I figured being single would be better for my running. I was okay for the first two weeks of our breakup, and then I got word that Mark was about to start dating someone else. Convinced it was actually over between us, I totally lost it. I stopped thinking clearly. I stopped thinking at all. I felt like my world was ending. I was in pain, and the pain had to end. I went into the bathroom, took a razor, and cut my wrists. It turns out, I was bad at killing myself. There was blood everywhere, but the cuts were very shallow and I was still very much alive. Desperate and scared, I did what came naturally to me. I called Mark. "You need to get over here," I said.

"What are you talking about, Suzy?" he said, sounding annoyed.

"I did something bad," I said.

He hung up and hurried over. When he saw me, he thought I'd hurt myself just to get his attention. He was used to thinking of me as happy and healthy, and so he wasn't able to understand that I might be genuinely suicidal or even mentally ill. But he was certainly worried about me. He held me in his arms, and I started to cry.

"Please let's get back together," I begged him over and over again.

"We'll talk about it," he said, "and try to work things out."

I was so relieved. I kept crying, but now they were tears of joy. And just a few days later, we did in fact get back together.

AFTER MARK AND I HAD been dating for several years, I began to relax and trust in our relationship. His love and support were good for me. When I first went away to college, I had thought I would visit my family often, but I found myself more and more absorbed by my new life with Mark. For the first time in my life, I wasn't putting my family's happiness before my own. But I still wanted, badly, to win for them, for my school, and for my home state. I'd begun to feel more confident in myself off the track, but I was still a wreck when it came time to race.

It also helped that I was working with Peter, the greatest coach I would ever have. I grew so much under his leadership, and trusted him completely. His style of coaching was different than that of his American counterparts. He knew it was important for his runners to learn to compete against international athletes as early in their competitive careers as possible, in order to have a shot at the Olympics. Because of this, he convinced the university to pay for the team to travel to Europe to race in the summer between school years. These experiences broadened my horizons and increased my confidence. When it came time to compete, Peter was all business. But when we first arrived in Europe and were simply training and acclimating ourselves to the different conditions, he relaxed and let his guard down considerably. He took us mountain climbing, and during a break in our hike, he pulled out his harmonica and played us a song. When he ran out of gas another day, he left us alone in a small village while he went off in search of fuel. Although we didn't speak the language, we enjoyed exploring and interacting with the town's residents. One night, he even dropped us off at a discotheque, so we could have some fun and soak up a little local culture. After a week, the other girls flew home, and I stayed behind with Peter to compete in several European races. When I saw that I could actually hold my own against the best runners in the world, it began to feel like all of my hard work was actually paying off. I continued to win at home, too, and not only regular track events, but every national track championship I entered during my college career—nine in all, at the time, the most NCAA championships for any athlete.

Now Mark and Peter had taken my dad's place as the important men in my life, but my father remained devoted to my running. He traveled to campus for all of my home meets, and to most of my away meets as well, and expected me to call him after every race—even those in other countries—to tell him the outcome and details. Having to balance his demands with my devotion to my coach and my boyfriend was not easy. But I couldn't break away. I still wanted to make him happy, and so I did as my father wished.

Luckily, this was a happy period in my family. Dan's doctors had found a cocktail of medication that worked for him, and he was following their orders. He got sober around the age of twenty-seven, which also helped his overall well-being. He was employed, had a great girlfriend, and was living in a medium-size city about forty-five minutes from my parents. He maintained his creative energy, and he even used it to come to my rescue once in college. As usual, I had put off an assignment until the very last minute because I was too busy running, and now I needed to create a sculpture for an art class *the next day*. I was visiting my parents when Dan stopped by.

"Oh, I've got a great idea," he said.

I couldn't wait to see what he'd pull off on the fly. I knew it would be great. Dan found a piece of Styrofoam our dad had lying around and used an electric carving knife to carve a perfect three-dimensional fish. It was incredible. And my teacher thought so, too.

BY MY SENIOR YEAR, IT was clear that academics were not going to be a strong factor in my college career—believe it or not, my basketball theory class didn't turn me into a great philosopher—but I was going to manage to graduate. And my life outside the classroom was better than ever before.

That winter I was taking a sports psychology class, which I could have benefited from had I been open to it. One night, Mark picked me up from class around nine thirty. By this point, we were living together in an apartment off campus, and he often treated me to our idea of a nice meal after class—pizza or Kentucky Fried Chicken. That evening, Mark wanted to go to Pizzeria Uno, which was a fancy dinner for us, since that's where we'd had our first date. It was a thoughtful gesture, but Mark was always doing things like that for me.

The restaurant was nearly empty, and we relaxed into our booth and caught up on how our days had been. As usual, I was happy just to be with him.

The next thing I knew, Mark stood up for no apparent reason. I watched with curiosity as he got down on one knee by the booth. At that moment, I understood what was happening. I was already crying before he could pull out the ring.

"Suzy, will you marry me?" he said.

"Yes," I said, kissing him with tears pouring down my face.

Our waiter came by, saw the ring and my tears, and congratulated us.

"I probably should have done something more elaborate," Mark said as he got up.

"No, this was perfect."

I wasn't sure how Mom and Dad would feel about my getting married at this point in my life, but Mark had already called them and asked for their blessing, which blew me away.

I didn't even know that was a thing people did, but it was just another example of Mark's thoughtfulness. We went home and took turns calling our parents, who were all overjoyed with the news. It was just this beautiful evening from beginning to end, and when we fell into bed together that night, we made love knowing that this was the start of our real life together. The next day, I had to catch a flight to Indianapolis for the national indoor track championships. I was tired, of course, from my exciting evening. I waited for the van to take me to the airport, getting drenched but still floating from the night before. When the van finally pulled up, I had the biggest smile on my face. My teammates started laughing when they saw me.

"You're drenched! Why are you so happy?" one of my teammates called out.

I pulled my right hand out of my pocket and held it up. The van erupted into screams.

I was the favorite to win the indoor track nationals that year, and I did. After the race, a sportswriter interviewed me. "Were you nervous?" he asked.

Normally I would have been plagued by nerves, but not that day.

"You know what?" I said. "Nothing could have upset me or made me nervous today! I just got engaged."

My training with Coach Peter was really paying off. That January, I signed a six-figure, five-year contract with Reebok, which meant I was now a professional runner and getting paid to do what I loved most. At the time, it was common for the big athletic companies to approach the coaches at the universities with the top student athletes, and Reebok had brought a deal to Peter for me. Because I didn't have an agent at the time and Mark was studying American Institutions, in preparation for law school, he negotiated the terms for me in a pretty amazing deal. It was incredible for a runner just out of college and far surpassed the deal Nike had on the table for me. My father felt left out of the negotiation process, but I was desperate for independence from my dad and preferred to receive help from my future husband than my father. Still, I knew my family was extremely proud of me, as was Peter. But I felt that the size of my various endorsements meant that I was now expected to run even faster, and win even more, in order to prove that I was worth the value of the contracts.

A week after we graduated from college Mark and I got married in Madison. We'd planned every detail ourselves, and I loved that day so much because it was a total representation of who we were. The university let us get married in an alumni building right on Lake Mendota. Even though I had received the first installments from my Reebok contract, we were on a budget, especially because we'd invited 250 guests. The university gave us a great deal on food and went out of their way to make the day special. Mark made the wedding programs on his computer and printed them off at the local copy shop. I didn't realize it was customary to order flowers for the church, so we didn't have any, but it didn't matter. All of our friends from the baseball and track teams were there, and the men in the wedding party wore Reebok high-tops, donated by the person who'd signed me to my contract, who was also there. It was casual, to say the least, but it was beautiful in its simplicity, and an amazing day.

Mark's parents sent us to Hawaii for our honeymoon, and then we prepared to drive from Wisconsin out to Malibu. Mark would attend Pepperdine for law school, and I would train for my first Olympics the next year. I cried as we left Wisconsin, but as Mark predicted, my tears only lasted five minutes. It was time to go for the gold. I had wanted to leave Wisconsin before I'd even started college or met Mark, and now that my horizons had been expanded so much in the past four years, I was more than ready to go. I don't think I realized at the time how much Peter did to help my running through our day-to-day training, and so I figured it would be fine for him to send me workouts via fax, as we'd planned when I decided to move away. Any anxiety I felt had to do with my running, and how well I would or wouldn't live up to Reebok's expectations and find my place within the professional running world. But, for the moment, I was excited to see what would come next.

Chapter 5
CHASING GOLD

I loved Malibu right away. It was everything Wisconsin wasn't: perpetually sunny and warm and possessed of a casual, anything-goes vibe I instantly adopted as my own. Just as Mark had been attractive to me because he was so different from the men I'd grown up with, Malibu was a whole new world, and I loved it. Maybe I hadn't made it to UCLA for college as I'd dreamed, but now I was finally free to start living my own life, and I was going to do so in California.

We used the money from my Reebok contract and the endorsement deals I'd also signed with Proctor & Gamble (Pert Plus), Clairol, Blue Cross Blue Shield, and Kikkoman

Soy Sauce to put a down payment on a 1,300-square-foot house in a more affordable section of Malibu and soon settled into the laid-back beach lifestyle. Even though Mark was busy with law school and I was in training, with my sights set on the 1992 Olympics the following summer, we still managed to find time for nights out at our favorite restaurants and afternoons by the Pacific with friends. Having grown up in landlocked Wisconsin, I found the ocean mesmerizing and could spend hours walking along the shoreline, picking up shells and sea glass. And I loved to run down to the beach from our house as part of my daily training.

I was happier than I'd been in a long time. Best of all, I was free of the watchful eyes I'd constantly felt on me in Wisconsin. It was such a relief to get a break from always feeling that I had to be perfect, that everyone was watching me, that I was living for other people's happiness. I'd sensed that my father didn't completely support my decision to marry and move away. Of course, true to form, he'd never said anything outright, but there had been tension in the months leading up to our wedding and departure for California. I could sense that my dad felt that I didn't fully appreciate all he had done to support my career. It seemed he felt left behind, that I had replaced him with first Coach Tegen and then Mark. I didn't want to hurt his feelings, and I definitely didn't want to discuss them. It was easier to be far away. I was finally getting a taste of the independence that I had craved. The trouble is, I didn't know what to do with it. I didn't even know who I wanted to be. After having the Olympics in my sights for more than a decade, I'd be trying out for my first Olympic team in a year. But, for the first time since I started running, it wasn't my sole obsession. I didn't want to train constantly. I wanted to let go and live for once and enjoy our new life as newlyweds.

A few months after we arrived, I noticed that Peter seemed less engaged with my training and less interested in my opinion. Around the same time, I took a job as the assistant coach for the cross-country team at Pepperdine. The running coach there, Dick Kampmann, began taking over the workouts Peter sent me, making them his own. He was a more low-key coach, and his relaxed approach to running suited my new laid-back California lifestyle. As much as I knew Peter had done for me, I could feel the beginnings of burnout, and I wanted my life to contain more than just running. That summer of 1991, my success on the track was modest, but it seemed like I was getting more press and attention than ever. As we went into the Olympic trials in the spring of 1992, my image as the all-American golden girl brought all sorts of opportunities that went far beyond the track. I was approached about doing a line of fitness videos. And not only did I land on the cover of *Olympian* magazine and *Runner's World*, but I found myself in the pages of *Rolling Stone*, *Vogue*, *Cosmopolitan*, and *Elle*. I liked all the attention and I was having fun, for once in my life as a runner. The years of anxiety and self-doubt had taken their toll, and I was eager to push those feelings aside and bask in the glow of this new attention. I still loved to run, but the thrill of modeling and being a celebrity became more and more attractive to me. And Reebok, seeing all of the positive attention

I was garnering, liked what they were getting, even though I wasn't dominating on the track. When I was asked—via my Reebok boss—to pose for *Playboy*, I was excited, but I immediately knew I couldn't actually do it, not only because of how my family would react, but because in my mind, an all-American golden girl wouldn't do something like that. By this point, I was very aware of my brand, and I also turned down a deal from Miller Brewing Company.

Going into the 1992 Olympic trials, I was a favorite to make the team. Not only had I won a record nine NCAA championships as a college runner, but I was running for Reebok, and they'd launched a huge promotional campaign around me going into the trials. I'd also qualified for the final of the Olympic trials in 1988, but my insecurity and anxiety had made me so convinced I didn't belong on the team that I'd pulled out before the race. This time, there was no question I was a professional runner, but another problem presented itself.

I was nervous. This was what I had been working toward for most of my life. And to ratchet up the tension, among the competitors in my best event—the 1,500 meters—was my childhood idol Mary Decker Slaney. I couldn't believe I would be sharing a track with the woman who had always inspired me. I didn't know it, but I'd also be facing my future nemesis, Regina Jacobs, who I would regularly compete against throughout my professional career. It seemed like I was forever coming in second to her at U.S. Nationals, which messed with my mind to no end. No matter how hard I trained, she always had the ability to finish races strong in a way I often couldn't. I cannot say I was surprised when she tested positive for steroid use in 2003, validating my long-held suspicions.

As we lined up at the starting blocks the day of the Olympic trials finals, it was hard not to watch Slaney's pre-race ritual out of the corner of my eyes, even though I knew I had to focus on my own performance and quiet the jitters that could cause me to tighten up and choke midstride. Thankfully, when the gun went off, I was all instinct, all body, and my mind went quiet. This was the zone that I felt most comfortable in. I had been so focused on Mary Decker Slaney that I almost didn't notice when Regina Jacobs suddenly pulled ahead to win the race. She was followed by her former Stanford teammate PattiSue Plumer in second place. I was stunned, but then, there I was, crossing the finish line in third place, with Mary Decker Slaney actually finishing *after* me in fourth place. I had run faster than my hero. And, most important, I had made the Olympic team.

It was traditional for runners who earned a place on the team to be given an American flag and sent on a victory lap. As I jogged down the track, waving my flag, it was as if my feet were bouncing a few feet off the ground, I was so buoyant with happiness. And then, there was Mark, wrapping me in his arms. That might have been the best moment of my professional running career to date. Everything I had wanted since I was twelve had finally come true. I was going to the Olympics in Barcelona.

This was before cell phones, so as soon as we got back to our hotel room to get ready for the celebratory dinner hosted by my Reebok rep, I called home. My mom and dad had seen my race on TV and were overjoyed for me. That felt so good after all they had done to support my running and how much I had longed to make them proud. Since leaving Wisconsin, I'd missed many family dinners and holidays, which especially displeased my sisters, and made us grow further apart. At the time, I was so focused on my new life that I didn't really register their reaction. And since we never talked about anything as a family, it was easy to pretend nothing was wrong. My running trumped everything else in my life, distorting my view of what was important. After my sisters became moms, I felt I couldn't be around their kids as much as I would have liked for fear I might get sick and miss a race or training. I knew my siblings were excited for me, but none of them called me to say so, and I didn't think much about this omission. I also knew signs had already gone up in the gas stations and supermarkets of my hometown, congratulating me on my win and cheering me on to the Olympics. Unfortunately, such vocal support from my home state quickly turned my euphoria into a feeling of pressure, as my short-lived victory high was replaced by the greatest anxiety of my racing life. Now that I had accomplished my dream of making the Olympic team, I had to run in the Olympics and risk disappointing everyone who had believed in me and supported me along the way.

Sure that I wasn't training or running at the level of the world's best, I panicked. Peter agreed to meet me in Norbonne, France, where the U.S. Olympic track team was staging a prep site for the two weeks before the Olympics. I desperately tried to make up for lost time under his guidance.

But before I knew it, I had to leave him behind and travel on to the Olympics in Spain alone.

Not every athlete participates in the opening ceremonies because it means standing for hours, which is exhausting. But this was my first Olympics, and I wouldn't have missed the opportunity for anything. It felt amazing to be out on the field with the most elite athletes in America, all of us dressed in matching uniforms and basking in the culmination of years, even decades, of work. We were all big sports fans, of course, and so athletes kept popping away from where they were supposed to be standing with their team in order to go get their picture taken with someone they particularly admired. A seven-foot-tall man approached me, and as he smiled down at me, I recognized him as former Duke star basketball player Christian Laettner. He was there to play on what had been dubbed the "Dream Team."

"Hey, Suzy, I remember watching you at your NCAA race our senior year in college," he said. "Can I get a picture with you?"

"With me?" I said, laughing that a Dream Teamer could want a photo with *me*.

As we posed, he looked over to where his teammates stood, hulking above all of the regular-sized athletes. "Do you want to come meet the Dream Team?" he asked.

"Oh my gosh," I said. "Of course I do."

I felt a little nervous as we approached Charles Barkley, David Robinson, and Magic Johnson, but they were so incredibly nice, it quickly put me at ease.

"Suzy, I just saw you in that Pert Plus ad you did," Magic said.

What, Magic Johnson knew who I was?

He leaned down and kissed my cheek. *Mark is not going to believe this,* I thought, knowing what a huge Lakers fan he was and had turned me into.

By the night before my preliminary, all the good feeling I had experienced at the opening ceremony had evaporated, and I was back in the dark, extremely negative head space that plagued me during competition. In a panic going into the Olympics, I had redoubled my training with my college coach, Peter Tegen, but there was only so much we could do in that time. I knew I was in no condition to beat the world's best, and Peter was not with me, so he wasn't there to give me any final words of wisdom now. And I was without my security blanket, Mark. Per official rules, no spouses were allowed to stay at the Olympic Village, so he stayed with my boss from Reebok. Little did I know that the mood at the Olympic Village was more spring break than a focused training zone. The athletes who had already competed in their events were ready to *party,* and the building in which I was staying had the chaotic vibe of a college dorm, complete with loud music, drunken shouts, and laughter. I was shocked to learn that thousands of condoms are made available in the village each year, and the Olympians were apparently making good use of them. As the minutes ticked by, I lay in bed, listening to the chaos, growing more and more agitated about my race, and thinking about how the less sleep I got, the worse I would do. Images of my upcoming race flashed through my mind, only they were the inverse of the positive visualization exercises recommended by coaches. I saw myself failing again and again and again. Finally, it was time to get up. I don't think I slept at all that night. I was very tired and dazed. I would have rather done anything than run an Olympic race that day, but I didn't have a choice.

I started my pre-race ritual, warming up and stretching. By the time I took the bus over to the warm-up track, my head was plagued with the familiar litany: *Why can't my leg be broken? Why am I here?* I didn't have Peter or Mark, who wasn't allowed access to me, there to calm me down. Of course, I was so used to doing what I was supposed to do that it never would have occurred to me to tell Mark how nervous I was or tell him that I didn't want to run. I just pretended everything was fine, like I'd been doing for years, even though I felt absolutely terrible. I was thrumming with anxiety, to the point where I could barely focus on what was happening around me as I took my position. And then, I started running. I was putting on a good face, but I didn't feel like I belonged there among these elite runners. And then the worries flooded me. I tightened up with a lap and a half to go. I was living the nightmare that many runners have: my limbs became impossibly heavy, and it felt like I was dragging my arms and legs through quicksand. It was over, and I knew it. The other racers flew past. I finished last.

I was devastated. But the humiliation wasn't over. My parents had flown to Spain to watch me race, as had a benefactor from Wisconsin who had given me money to help pay for my training. My parents told me that he was expecting to have a meal with me, and I had to attend. The last thing I wanted to do was sit through a meal with a fake smile on my face while everyone tried to make me feel better, but I couldn't speak up. I went to lunch, suffering through the hour until I could go hide. I couldn't bear to go back to the Olympic Village, where I was sure everyone knew who I was and that I'd let down my team and my country by losing when I'd been expected to do more. That night, Mark and I went to sleep early on the floor of the hotel room rented by my Reebok liaison. We got up early in the morning while he was still asleep and went straight to the airport. My first Olympics were over.

Following my disappointment in Barcelona, I became aware of a rising backlash against me in the running world. I heard whispers that I wasn't good enough to attract all the money and attention I'd received going into the Olympics. Other female athletes criticized me for getting praised for my looks. I was making a lot of money, more than many of my peers who were running as fast or faster than I was, and they felt I was getting more attention than I deserved. All of this cut into my already shaky self-esteem. When I'd appeared on the cover of *Runner's World* the previous year, they'd severely airbrushed my photo, decreasing my bust size so I appeared flat chested, the way female runners were supposed to look. I hated that my breasts still drew attention to me and made me look anything other than the absolute ideal runner. That summer, I secretly paid eight thousand dollars for breast reduction surgery, even though the doctors warned me I might have trouble breast-feeding if I ever became a mother. Once I was healed, I was happy that at least I looked the way runners were supposed to look. But the surgery alone wasn't going to put me back in top form. As much as I'd enjoyed my time in the paradise that was Malibu and a brief escape from the normal intensity of my running life, I always thought my coaches and father expected more of me, and as long as I was disappointing them, I couldn't be happy anymore. Although I was not enjoying the competitive aspect of running, I wanted to win for others in my life, and so couldn't feel good unless I was winning again for them. I missed training with Peter the way we had when I was in college, and I longed to have a more involved coach again, but I wasn't ready to move back to Wisconsin. I wasn't performing as well as I should be, and that meant that I had to find a new coach who could help me to be the runner I knew I could be. Hopefully this would help me to find my love of running again. My thoughts immediately went to my longtime idol, Mary Decker Slaney, whose former coach, Dick Brown, was based in Eugene, Oregon. A good runner friend of mine trained with Dick and had suggested I give him a try. It would be a big change from Malibu. Mark still had a year of law school at Pepperdine left, but I didn't feel like I could wait. I moved to Eugene alone and we spent a semester apart, and then he finished up his law degree at the University of Oregon so he could be with me, always sacrificing for me and my running career.

The change was exciting, and I threw myself into a new regimen and life. My new coach had strong opinions about many aspects of my life, even those that I felt weren't directly related to my running. He grew irritated with my post-race ritual of calling my dad to tell him how I'd done, as my dad expected. He thought my dad was overly involved in my life, and he encouraged me to finally create the distance I'd long been craving. When my dad criticized me once for losing a race, Coach Brown was extremely upset.

I continued to be a natural pleaser who found comfort in being told what to do—by my father, my coaches, and my husband. But Coach Brown took this further. One day, after he'd led me through my usual series of sprints and my weight routine, he sat down with me. He was a micromanager, and I assumed we were going to talk about technique or new training goals.

"Suzy, there's something I've been wanting to talk to you about," he said.

"What's that?" I asked, eager to do whatever he asked.

"It's about your performance," he said. "If you really want to race well, you're going to have to stop having sex before races."

I looked down quickly, blushing. Even though Mark and I continued to have a loving and adventurous sex life, this conversation with my *coach* was way beyond my comfort level.

"I don't know what you mean," I said.

"I mean you need all of your energy to race. When you have sex, you deplete your testosterone levels, which you need to perform. I don't want any of that testosterone to go to waste. So no sex the day before a race. Or the day of. I'm your coach. I know what's best for you."

"Okay," I said, nodding, too embarrassed to look up.

I felt myself curl up inside, awkward and uneasy in my own body, like I had been when the male coach had been caught videotaping my breasts, or when Coach Peter told me about the letter recommending I wear two sports bras. I'd been so uncomfortable about the unwanted attention that I'd had a breast reduction. But nothing was enough. My body wasn't mine. It belonged to my sport. My coach. Magazine editors. My peers.

Mark picked me up from practice as usual that day, and as soon as I was in the car with him, I told him what Coach Brown had said.

"You've got to be fucking kidding me," Mark said.

I sighed and looked out the window. I missed Malibu and the beach and our friends. I was working so hard, only to be devastated by anxiety and the constant assessment of every part of my life and body. I wanted to be invisible.

Once again, my best friend Mary came to my rescue. Mary had given up running in college when she realized she didn't have the passion to do everything that went into competing at the professional level. She was now a successful lobbyist. Even still, she came to my meets when she could. That summer she flew to Europe to watch me run and enjoy some time abroad with us. It only took her a few days to get a handle on something that had been nagging at me for months. She didn't speak to me directly because she knew how personal a runner's relationship with her coach is, but while she and Mark were sitting on the beach in Monte Carlo, she told him that she couldn't understand why I was working with Coach Brown. She thought he was terrible for me because of the way he smothered me. As soon as Mark told me what Mary had said, I knew she was right. But changing coaches was a big deal. We'd made a major move to Eugene, and another big move seemed daunting. Plus, my results had improved from what they'd been in Malibu.

Even though I wasn't happy, I kept my head down and kept my sights on the 1996 Olympics in Atlanta.

I was overjoyed to qualify for the team again, although Dick had me compete in two events—the 800 and the 1,500, a decision I questioned, and I only made the team for the 800. Although the 1,500 was my specialty, I had run out of gas going into the final after running six rounds in less than a week, and finished last. To be honest, I didn't have particularly high expectations for the Atlanta games, but I tried to focus on the fact that I had made my second Olympic team. And then that June, the unthinkable happened: my longtime idol and Coach Brown's former athlete, Mary Decker Slaney, was suspended by the International Amateur Athletic Federation on suspicion of using performance-enhancing drugs. Even though her suspension was later lifted, the scandal cast a shadow over her reputation as a runner. I couldn't believe she might have taken drugs. I knew they were everywhere in the sport, and I'd long struggled to keep a positive attitude about being beaten by runners who were giving performances that seemed like they must be drug enhanced.

I didn't win in Atlanta. I wasn't surprised, but I was still disappointed. Once again the whisper campaign started. I wasn't living up to all the hype. Reebok was thinking about bringing an end to their sponsorship of runners, which would mean cutting me, and Nike didn't seem overly interested. The public only cared about track during the Olympics, and I had never won a medal. I wondered if I was being naïve about drugs. I'd always vowed to run clean, but maybe that was a mistake.

When we got back to Eugene, I sat down with Coach

Brown. "Am I missing the boat here?" I said. "Should I be using drugs? Everybody seems to be doing them."

He held my gaze for a long time, letting me know how serious he was.

"You are absolutely not going to do drugs," he said. "You don't need them. You're talented enough."

I was relieved. I didn't want to break the rules. I was a good girl. But, still, I wondered what I needed to do to win.

"I guess I'm just a little frustrated with where our training is going, then," I said. "I sometimes just don't think it's intense enough."

He quickly reassured me, outlining a scientific plan for a new approach to our workouts that would bring my performance to a higher level. But I'd heard this from him before, and I'd never seen the results I'd been promised. I wanted, needed, to win. I should have pushed back this time, but I wasn't strong enough for that.

In 1996, I was approached about doing a swimsuit calendar, and I immediately loved the idea. Even though I'd been self-conscious about my large breasts before my surgery, I was comfortable showing off my body off the track. I'd even gone topless on a beach in Europe when I competed there, although Mark worried the whole time that I'd be spotted and photographed, leading to a scandal, and so I finally put my top back on at his urging. I wanted to do something that would make me feel good, for a change, when racing wasn't doing it for me. I loved every aspect of putting the calendar together, from the shoot on a beach in Hawaii, which the entertainment news show *Extra* sent a crew to cover, to the process by which we chose the twelve photos we would use for the calendar. When I received boxes of the finished product, I was proud that I'd finally created something I'd enjoyed and was an expression of my personality. The calendar wasn't available in retail stores, but we advertised it a bit, and it became an instant success. We quickly sold out of the five thousand copies we'd printed, and it seemed like we could sell as many again if we printed more. And then our phone rang. It was Dad.

"What is going on with this ridiculous swimsuit calendar of yours?" he growled into the phone. "I didn't even know anything about it, and suddenly, I'm getting teased at work. You've really embarrassed me."

"Dad, this is something I wanted to do," I said, even though I felt queasy standing up to my father. "I love to model."

He was angry and embarrassed, believing the calendar reflected poorly on our family, and I was feeling worse by the minute. I'd finally found something I really enjoyed, and now my dad was taking all the joy away.

"I wonder if I was a stripper, Dad," I said, "would you disown me?"

He didn't answer the question. By the time I hung up the phone, I was anxious and depressed and feeling plenty of guilt. When Mark came home not long after, I was still crying.

"What's wrong?" he asked.

"My dad called and he's really angry about my swimsuit calendar," I said. "He wants me to stop doing it."

Mark had been completely supportive of the entire project, even helping me to pick out the swimsuits I was photographed in, and he paused now before taking a side.

"You loved doing the calendar," he said. "And it's doing really well. If we print an additional ten thousand, I'm sure we can sell them out. But it's your call."

Within a few days, I stopped selling the calendar. I still couldn't bear to make my father unhappy. But I was angry about his reaction and the fact that I'd caved to his pressure. And so, even though I wasn't strong enough to fully rebel, I did pull back from my parents even more. And this was a crucial moment for me to do so because Mark and I had decided to make another major change. Every time I got tempted to focus on something other than running, like modeling or public appearances, they took me away from what I was here to do: run fast. It was time to double down on my training. Modeling was flattering and fun. But at the same time I still wanted to win. The inner conflict was tearing me up.

Although the next Olympics were still three and a half years away, I was going to show the world what I could do. I'd been a professional runner for six years, but I hadn't achieved anything like the success I'd had in college. And I knew there was only one man who could get me back to the competitive level I'd been at then: my old coach, Peter Tegen. For some reason, training with him long distance never worked as well as it did when we were on the track together. It was time to go home. It was scary for me to be moving close to my parents again, just as our relationship had grown more strained. Such tension was one of the reasons I'd left in the first place, and the physical distance between us had felt like a good thing to me. But Mark really felt the move was what I needed, if success on the track was my goal, and I eventually agreed. I was sick of hearing the whispers about how I wasn't living up to expectations. I was sick of mediocrity. I wanted to win.

In early 1997, we moved back to Madison. Immediately, Peter and I fell back into our old rapport, and my running began to improve. I had a great year in 1997, winning in Paris and Lausanne. And then, in 1998, I had one of the best running moments of my life, competing in one of my favorite venues: the Hercules Meet in Monte Carlo. Because of the upswing in my career, Nike had finally come calling, and they'd written a clause into my contract stating that if I could run 1,500 meters in under four minutes, I'd receive a one-hundred-thousand-dollar bonus. The race happened to fall on my thirtieth birthday. I didn't win the race. I came in eighth, actually. But I ran it in a personal best, 3:59, which meant I'd earned my sub-four-minute time bonus, and I felt like I was back where I wanted to be, running the best I could at that point, holding my own with the top athletes in the world.

My happiness didn't last long. That night, while I was attending a post-race celebration party, the meet promoter for one of the most prestigious meets in the world pulled me aside for a private conversation.

"You could change the sport of track and field," he said.

"Thank you," I said, feeling proud.

"I mean it. With everything you've done with your modeling and the press you've received, you could really help the sport in America. But you have to do better. You have to win, and to do that, you know what you have to do."

My smile instantly faded. I stepped back from him a little, tears forcing their way out. I was shocked and offended by what he'd just said without saying it: in order to be the best, I had to use steroids. If I did, I could change a sport I loved dearly. If I didn't, it was my fault if I lost.

"Excuse me," I said, wishing Mark were there to defend me, as I pushed away from him and into the crowd. I never spoke to him again.

The problem with being a top athlete is that there's always another race, and no matter how many times you've won before, you have to keep winning to maintain your reputation. The next year, 1999, was a rough year for me. I tore my Achilles tendon in an early indoor race in Boston while setting the indoor American record in the 800 meters. I missed the rest of the '99 season and was initially told by my doctors that my career might be over. I was determined to run and prove them wrong.

I'd continued to maintain some distance from my parents following their disapproval of my swimsuit calendar. But when I did go to their house for a visit, it was impossible not to notice how my brother's condition had changed, although my parents didn't discuss the subject. We didn't know it at the time but, after years of hanging on to his mental health, he'd stopped taking his meds. This had allowed him to lose at least forty pounds, and he looked better than he had in years. Both Mark and I couldn't help but compliment him when we saw him at my parents' house at the end of the summer. What we later learned was that his decision to go off his medication was a part of a downward spiral that would cause him to give his money and belongings away, paint graffiti all over his house and car, and then take his own life on September 9, 1999.

I was shocked of course. We all were. None of us had thought his illness would ever really lead to this. That fateful day had felt a little strange to begin with, and although I'd gone to train at the university gym with a friend, I paused in my workout to call Mark, which I never did. When I was training, I was training. When Mark heard my voice on the phone there was a long silence. After what seemed like an hour, Mark finally spoke.

"Suzy, it's your brother."

As soon as I heard these words, and the tone of voice with which Mark spoke them, somehow I knew Dan had died.

"Dan's gone."

I dropped the phone and fell to my knees in the coach's office, where I had gone to make my call. When I picked up the phone again, I had just one question.

"Why? Why did this happen?" I asked again and again.

"Suzy, you need to get home," Mark said.

As I sobbed, he talked me through a plan where I would return to the gym, tell my friend what had happened and follow her to my house in my car, where Mark waited for me, so she could be sure I made it home safely. During the half-hour drive, my tears dried up, and I became like a zombie, totally checked out from reality and the pain it contained.

As usual, I went into my default mode. I trained, or cross-trained at least. As soon as my brother's funeral was over, I left for the airport to fly to Albany for an appearance I'd promised to make at a fundraiser in honor of a young girl who'd passed away, and then to Limerick for a much-anticipated miracle treatment I needed for my Achilles, skipping the reception my parents had planned at their house. My relationship with my sisters was already tense, and this was the final straw for them. They went off on me, telling me I was selfish, putting another family's loss and my career before my family. But I didn't know what else to do, and even when I tried to explain this to my sisters, they wouldn't listen. Following the surgery I'd required on my Achilles, I hadn't run pain-free in nearly a year, and I couldn't stand it anymore. I needed to do something to feel better. I needed to run. I limped through my physical therapy in Ireland, constantly thinking about my brother's final moments as he'd jumped off a nine-story building to his death. I was haunted. Desperate, I attended church in Ireland, where I was made to feel very welcome. This helped, as did the letter I received telling me that my appearance in Albany had been very healing for the community. Slowly, I began to recover from the devastating loss of my brother, but his death still left a hole in my heart.

The intensely painful treatment worked. When I was finally well enough to start racing again in 2000, Mark suggested I dedicate that whole season to my brother's memory and add Favor back to the name under which I competed. It felt like the least I could do.

The shadow of Dan added another layer to an already high-stakes year for me. I was thirty-two years old, and it would be my third attempt at the Olympics. Mark and I had been married for almost ten years but had put off having a family. I felt like I had to finally make good on all the sacrifices that Mark, my parents, and my coaches had made for so many years. I had to win.

After the severity of my injury the previous year, it was amazing that I was running at all. But I didn't take that into consideration as I geared up for the 2000 European season after qualifying for the Olympic team by coming in second—of course, to Regina Jacobs—at the Olympic trials in the 1,500 meters. I had pushed my training harder than ever, feeling like I had so much to make up for—my past two Olympic disappointments, the pain my family was experiencing over the death of my brother. If I could just bring home a gold medal, we'd at last have something to be happy about.

A runner can typically peak only once in a season, so coaches try to have this peak at the time of the season's biggest race, after which it's difficult to run quite so fast because of natural wear and tear and physical and psychological exhaustion. That year, I was running great—too great, actually. I peaked in Europe just after the Olympic trials, running my career best, and a seasonal world's fastest, in the 1,500 meters, 3:57, in Oslo, and establishing myself as the favorite in Sydney. This was just a couple tenths of a second off the American record set years before by Mary Decker Slaney. Although I injured my hamstring soon after and missed two weeks of training, there was nothing to do but keep running, especially because I was the favorite for the 2000 Olympics, and Nike had me shoot a major television commercial just before I left for Sydney. Unfortunately, the commercial itself was met with criticism—from my mom, who thought that the portrayal of me running from an attacker reflected badly on our family, given Dan's death by suicide, and from some feminists, who condemned what they claimed was a message of violence against women. I thought that the message was a positive one: I could escape a killer without needing a man to come to my rescue. Even so, the money had been spent, and I felt pressure from Nike to make good by winning in Sydney. Not only that, but I wanted to win so badly for my family. I had a gold-or-bust attitude; anything less than the best would be a complete failure.

Things were shaky from the start. I had two rounds before my Olympic final, and while I won the first round, I only felt okay, not great. In the second round, I came in second, but it was not as easy as it should have been, and I felt terrible, like I'd already spent everything. I knew I was in trouble for my final race two days later. I wanted to flee. I followed the other runners in a single file line through the tunnel from the locker room, a television cameraman close by my side. Even with a huge fake smile plastered on my face, I was worried the camera would capture my lack of confidence somehow. My brain started swirling with negative thoughts and doubts. The crowd was so loud. I glanced at the people in the stands, cheering. *Stay focused,* I thought. Then my eyes darted around at my competitors. *Can they see the fear in my eyes?* I wondered. *Why can't this be over? Why don't I just pull out of the race?* I wanted so badly to silence my critics, but I was such a mental mess that I just didn't feel like I had it in me. I looked to the area of the stands where I knew Mark was cheering me on, wishing he would come down to the track and rescue me. I felt so alone that I felt my throat clog with suppressed tears. *I can't cry. I have to run. I can't let him down. He has given up so much of his career for me and this moment. My family is watching, too. I have to win for them. It would bring so much joy to them after my brother's suicide. I could help take away some of the pain. Focus, Suzy, focus.*

The official called us all to get on the starting line. I was assigned to be the first runner, closest to the inside rail of the track. This meant I had to get off to a fast start in order to avoid getting boxed in by my competitors. I adjusted the blue sunglasses that matched my USA Olympic uniform, a nervous habit, wishing the cameraman would get his lens out of my face. I shook both legs out, patted the numbers on the side of my uniform so they wouldn't fall off. *Why are they holding us so long at the start? Can't we get this over?* My heart felt as if it was going to pound itself to dust, and I hadn't started running. Then the gun went off, and the sound was so loud, it echoed in my head as I took my first strides. My newly sharpened spikes gripped the track's surface. Around me, everyone was pushing to get into the position needed to win the race. I tried to push my way in, too, focusing on the strategy Peter had drilled into me. But with every stride, the only thought in my head was *I just want this nightmare to be over.*

After running three laps in sheer panic, I had one more lap to go. But the closer I got to the finish line the more certain I became that something terrible was going to happen, any second. The gusty exhales of the runners behind me grew louder, making me feel like I was being hunted like an animal in the wild. My body turned to stone. I couldn't take another step. But I had to. I wanted to vanish, just disappear, but there was nowhere to go. I tried to hold on, but the tornado of negative thoughts and doubts was spinning through my brain faster and faster. My legs grew heavier and heavier, and with 150 meters left, one by one, the other runners passed me, until there was no one left but me. I was going to come in last, in my last Olympic race. No gold for Mark, no gold for Peter, no gold for my parents, no gold for my brother's memory. Heartbroken, panicked, almost dumb with grief, I just stopped. I told myself to fall, and then, I fell. Feeling the track against the bare skin of my arms and legs, I felt like such an idiot, a fuck-up, but at least I didn't have to run anymore. And then I realized I was still far from the finish line, and I couldn't leave this race unfinished. I forced myself up onto my feet and made myself finish, but when I saw the media crowding around me, I couldn't bear the shame of what I'd just done, and I collapsed again. It was over. I closed my eyes, woozy with emotion and exertion, and felt the medics lift me off the ground and into the air.

◆ ◆ ◆

Untreated bipolar disorder is a ticking time bomb waiting to go off. No matter how much a person might love the high of the manic episodes when they come or might want to climb out of the lows in order to feel better, function normally, and even be happy, this is not a condition that can be self-regulated. This is not a matter of goal setting or positive thinking or getting some rest. Studies show that 15 to 17 percent of those whose bipolar disorder goes untreated ultimately die by suicide. And that's only the cost that can be measured. Not to mention the sufferers who, without realizing their brain chemistry is driving them to do so, turn to drugs, alcohol, sex, shopping, anything to quiet the torment of their rushing mind. And in so doing, lose jobs, destroy marriages, break up families, all the while being blamed for their reckless behavior, as if they had any choice in the matter.

Even my brother, Dan, who was diagnosed relatively early, when he was still in high school, and treated with electroshock therapy and medication, still became a casualty of the disease. Of course, back then, getting the diagnosis wasn't the same as gaining an understanding of what it meant. Learning that Dan was bipolar in no way prepared my family or me for the struggles he would face in his too-short lifetime. I first learned of Dan's specific diagnosis not long after he received it. But, at the time, I was too young to understand what bipolar disorder was. When his behavior was at its most destructive—and painful for my family—I resorted to the easy slurs of the day, calling him crazy in my mind and wishing he would just snap out of it so my mom would stop crying. Looking back, I'm embarrassed by my own ignorance and regretful that I didn't have the same knowledge I do now. But I still had so much to learn back then, and unfortunately, I would have to learn it the hard way.

Chapter 6
REAL LIFE

The stress of the race itself was over, but the nightmare went on and on. As far as I was concerned, this was the worst thing that had ever happened to me, worse than any other loss, worse, even, than my brother's death. My perceptions were totally distorted. I was a wreck.

The incident was big news; I was a veteran runner and the visual of me collapsing onto the track was dramatic, even haunting. In the immediate aftermath, Mark was terrified I'd really injured myself. And the media were clamoring for an interview. So I lied. To my husband, to journalists, to my coach, to everyone but the only person who knew the truth of the matter: myself. I pretended I had fallen, when I knew

I had collapsed just to end the ordeal. The medic who treated me immediately after the race cited dehydration as the cause of my collapse, and so I gratefully went with that excuse, even though, as careful as I was with my training, I never would have allowed dehydration to befall me like that. During subsequent exams, it was revealed that I had a broken ischium bone, which had been the cause of the hamstring pain that had kept me from training adequately in the weeks leading up to Sydney. This injury had also contributed to my fall, at least in terms of the psychological toll it had taken on me. Any elite runner could have been thrown off by such a setback, and for me, it had been psychologically debilitating.

I was embarrassed and heartbroken. In my mind, I had failed not only myself, but also Peter, who had devoted so much to me, and I hadn't even made good by winning him a gold. I felt the whole world viewed me as a failure, which was devastating after two decades of nonstop training and competition based on the idea that I had the potential to be the best.

In the wake of my fall, I couldn't get home fast enough, but once we were back in Madison, I couldn't bring myself to leave my house. Upon arriving home to our small town of New Glarus, we drove under a big banner that said something along the lines of, GREAT JOB, SUZY! It was well intentioned, but only added to my sense of embarrassment. When I went to the grocery store, I was sure everyone was staring at me, whispering behind my back about how I had failed and let down our whole state—no, our whole country—so I stopped leaving the house. I wanted the whole event to go away. It was months before I didn't think about what had happened almost constantly. Mark was concerned about me and encouraged me to get out of the house and go running, which he knew would be more therapeutic for me than anything else, and spend time with our friends. But he didn't press me. I did a good job of hiding the true extent of my anxiety and shame from him, and even though I'd always leaned on him for advice and support, when it came down to it, he'd been conditioned to go along with whatever I said was best for my training, and so he didn't intervene now.

At the urging of an incredible doctor I'd found during our time in L.A., I finally forced myself to go see a sports psychologist for the first time in my career, in order to discuss what had happened. But even in the safety of her office, I was never really honest. I told her that I had fallen on purpose, but I didn't reveal just how dark my mental state had been going into the race. She decided the fall in Sydney was due to the extreme stress of having so much riding on a single race, and nothing in our discussions led her to suspect there was any more to it.

When the dust finally cleared, it was time to take stock of my running career and of the life Mark and I had built together since our marriage. I didn't want to race anymore. I was terrified that the minute I strapped on my spikes I'd be crippled with panic. But I was too proud to end my career on such a low note. I rallied, kept training, and in 2001 things were on the upswing again. I actually had quite a good year in 2001. Or at least I had a good *running* year. My life continued to be dictated by my obsessive focus. I spent most of my time with my coach, Peter, and Mark. In his dual role as my husband and part-time manager, Mark was aware of my every move. I had remained close to Mary, even though she had married an old contact of mine from Nike we'd set her up with and moved to Portland to be with him. We talked on the phone frequently and saw each other as often as we could. Later that year, she called me with terrible news.

"Suzy, I have to tell you something," she said, slowly and quietly.

"What is it?" I asked, instantly worried because it was unlike her to sound so serious. I was sitting at the kitchen table drinking tea, and I looked up at Mark, who was standing across from me.

"I have cancer," she said, her voice shaking. "But don't worry, I'm going to fight it, and I'm going to win."

My heart tightened up and tears rolled down my face.

If anyone could beat cancer, it was Mary, who was still the most dynamic, charismatic force of nature I'd ever known. But her diagnosis—a rare cancer—and ensuing need for a particularly intense form of chemotherapy meant she had a hard battle ahead. I made a point to get to Portland several times that year to be with my dear friend. She always amazed me with her energy and good spirits, even when she was sick, and it was easy to pretend she'd be back to normal in no time. Plus, I knew that was what Mary wanted, and wanted me to believe.

I had a great season in 2002, running three 1,500s under four minutes and earning a ranking of number three in the world. My training was going so well that I began looking toward competing in one more Olympics, in 2004. But as the trials approached, my nagging injuries began to get the best of me. I was traveling to Limerick once a month for deep-tissue treatment, and also making trips to Germany for injections to remove scar tissue. My body was telling me. enough. Although I had run through worse injuries many times, I was worried about my mental state more than my physical body. I was terrified of what might happen if I tried to race when I knew I wasn't at my best. I pulled my hamstring during the preliminary round of the Olympic trials, and I just didn't have it in me to push through the pain and the fear. I had learned something from Sydney at least. So I pulled out of the final race.

Mark and I had been talking seriously about starting a family. We'd both always wanted children, and now that we had a space in our life that running used to fill, it seemed like the perfect moment to welcome a child. When I found out I was pregnant in early 2005, we were overjoyed. I loved being pregnant and couldn't wait to be a mother. Mark and I were living in Blanchardville then, a small town thirty minutes outside of Madison. Our house was timber framed and cozy, nestled in a grove of grand oaks and maples on sixty-plus acres of woodland that included a creek and a running trail Mark had made for me. I continued to run through the woods daily during my pregnancy, but I was glad to be focused on picking baby names and getting our daughter's room ready. I had yet to officially announce I was retiring, but as soon as I announced I was pregnant, people in the running world and my own family assumed I would retire, or at least take a break, in order to become a mom. My parents were overjoyed to be grandparents again, and their focus on my running was soon transferred to their excitement about their new granddaughter.

I pretty much knew it was time to put my dream on the shelf. Many athletes have a hard time retiring, because without the daily routine of training to give their life structure, and the positive reinforcement of winning to make them feel like they have value, they become depressed, or worse. This was not the case for me. I had hated competing for decades, since high school really, and had been looking forward to retiring for years. My demons had taken me down in Sydney. Any joy I had ever experienced in competition, and there hadn't been much, was gone, never to return. I didn't want to be a runner anymore. I still ran every day, but not with the need to complete the same number of miles, or with the same intensity, day after day. It was a huge relief. I loved lacing up my sneakers to go for a mellow ten-mile run. I was thrilled to have a break from the exhausting nonstop cycle of training and traveling, and then training some more. It was time to do something else.

Mark and I had begun to make a tentative plan that he would practice law, and once I was ready to return to work, I would coach, do motivational speaking, and make appearances, or some combination of the three. Life in Wisconsin was less expensive, and we had no reason to worry about supporting ourselves. The transition seemed likely to be an easy one. I did have to make one difficult trip that year when I visited Mary at her new house in Boston. I had seen her several times since she'd been diagnosed with cancer, and she'd filled me with hope with her resolve to get well. This time, things were different, though. I knew it as soon as she came to the door to welcome me on the first day of my visit. Mary had lost a lot of weight, as well as her thick brown hair, from the chemo, and she looked extremely frail. When I hugged her, I was alarmed to feel her bones through her skin. But then we pulled back and looked at each other, and she flashed her great crooked grin, and it was just like old times again.

I stayed with Mary for several days, and during that time, she insisted on taking a walk with me every day, even though she had to go slowly. This was such a change from our freshman year, when we ran so fast on the track that our teammates complained. Mary was still so young, only thirty-seven years old, and I wanted to believe in her. As we walked, our pace began to match, our arms swinging lightly by our sides, and our hands found each other, the fingers linking.

"How's Mark?" she asked.

"He's so excited to be a dad," I said. "And I know he's going to be great."

"Mark was born ready to be a dad," she joked.

That was Mary, always making me laugh.

"He's definitely always been a lot more mature than me," I said. "You know, I still feel really bad that I wasn't able to make it to your wedding. It would have meant so much to me to be there."

"You were racing," Mary said. "If anyone should get that, it's me. I wish you could have been there, too, though. It was the happiest day of my life. I feel so lucky that Fred came into my life when he did. He really is my guardian angel. Especially now."

It felt so normal, talking about boys like we always had, even though now those boys were men—our husbands—and I was about to become a mom, an experience Mary was hoping for once she completed her cancer treatment, having put aside some of her eggs. But by the time we got back to Mary's house, her already slow pace was flagging, and she had to stop and rest before she was able to climb the stairs to her front door. I reached for her arm to help her, but she leaned on the railing instead, independent as always. By the time we got inside, Mary felt ready to lie down. But she had something else she wanted to do. When we walked into the living room, she unrolled her yoga mat on the floor and had me sit down on the floor near her. We both crossed our legs and placed our palms together in front of our hearts.

"Okay, close your eyes," she said, leading me through a simple introduction to yoga. "Slow your breathing."

I knew that yoga, and especially the meditation component, had become incredibly important to Mary during her cancer treatment. I knew she loved it and I was eager to support anything that made her feel better. But the whole thing was quite a mystery to me. I was able to slow my breathing, but not my mind, which raced ahead at a million thoughts a moment, just like it always did. I followed along as best I could as Mary led me through several basic poses, but as soon as she brought our session to a close, I popped up off the floor, needing to be back in motion. Mary, on the other hand, was more than ready for her afternoon nap. An hour later, I found myself sitting on the couch, staring into space, a magazine discarded next to me. I'd never been much of a reader, and I really couldn't concentrate now. All I could think about was Mary, how she'd always been my idol because of her style, independence, and zest for life. She just had to beat her cancer. She just had to. I stood and quietly tiptoed into her room to check on her. It was hard to see her, she looked so small in her bed, her thin limbs barely raising the blankets that covered her. I stopped short. The room wasn't just completely quiet; it was full of peace, a palpable energy that was warm and golden like sunlight. I smiled through my tears, thinking how lucky I was to have this exceptional friend. If anyone could beat cancer, it was Mary.

I LOVED EVERYTHING ABOUT BEING pregnant, and I even loved giving birth, thanks to a well-timed epidural. I was so aware of everything in that moment, as if the preciousness of it all heightened my experience and brought everything into the sharpest focus. Kylie was born six weeks before her due date, and even though my doctor had told me there was nothing to worry about, it was hard not to fear that something might go wrong until I finally saw her and knew that she was healthy.

When Mark first saw Kylie, his face was filled with the glow of so much love. A nurse helped Mark cut the umbilical cord and place Kylie in my arms. All the love and joy within me rushed up to the surface, overwhelming me, and I began to cry. I looked up at Mark, who was beaming down at us and crying, too. My eyes returned to Kylie. I couldn't stop looking at her. She was so beautiful, perfect, with the cutest little nose and cheeks.

"My little peach," I said, leaning forward to kiss her sweet face.

Everything I had done in my life before Kylie, save marrying Mark, seemed so small in that moment. Mark and I had created a miracle. I looked up at him again and we locked eyes, both smiling and crying at the same time, totally in the moment together.

Because she was born prematurely, Kylie had to stay in the hospital for ten days, which was hard for me. I just wanted to take her home to our little house in the woods, where I could care for her and we could begin our life together as a family. As my doctors had warned, I couldn't breast-feed because of my reduction surgery. I wanted to feel as close to my daughter as possible, and it was hard not to fear I was failing her because my body wouldn't do what it was supposed to do. From there, things got worse. Once Kylie finally came home, my fears amplified. I loved her. I loved her so much. I loved her so much that I couldn't put her down. I literally could not bear the intense anguish of separation I experienced every time I set her down in her swing or her bassinet, even when she was sound asleep and didn't notice I wasn't holding her anymore. My brain started to spin and whirl like it used to when I was a little girl and needed to do something, anything—cleaning the house, mowing the lawn, or running, of course—to calm it down. When Kylie napped, I ran up and down the hill behind our house with the baby monitor in my hand, pushing myself as hard as I could. The only thing that made me feel better was to sit on the couch with Kylie in my arms, but even that wasn't enough to recalibrate my brain.

I stopped eating, except for protein shakes and Pop-Tarts, and as had happened before, eating less gave me this strange serenity, like I finally had control over at least one aspect of my life. I lost the twenty-six pounds I'd gained during my pregnancy very quickly, and still, I didn't start eating more. And still, I didn't feel normal. I knew something was wrong, but I didn't know what.

One day, when Kylie went down for her morning nap, I set her in her bassinet and went into the kitchen to make myself a protein shake. As I stood at the counter, a rush of profound anguish overcame me, and I started to cry. All I wanted was to hold my precious little girl, who needed me, and I went back into her room and picked her up, rocking her in my arms on the couch for the rest of the day. When Mark came in from work that night, he found me sitting exactly where I'd been when he left in the morning, with Kylie in my arms.

"Hi, honey, how's our little girl?" he asked.

"She's perfect," I said, looking down at her sweet little face.

"Did you have a chance to make those phones calls that I asked you to?" he asked.

"No, I didn't," I said, my voice rising at anything I interpreted as criticism from him, unable to see my own hypersensitivity.

Mark looked at me with concern, and I tried to smile.

"It's okay," he said. "I'll make them on my way into town tomorrow."

We had scenes like this often during those first few months after Kylie was born, and as Mark's worry grew, he tried to find little ways to help me. One morning, instead of rushing off to the office or a meeting with a client, he lingered over a cup of tea at the dining room table, while I held Kylie, as usual.

"Why don't you let me take Kylie for a little while so you can go for a run? That always makes you feel better."

Just the thought of handing over Kylie, even for an hour, made me nearly choke with panic, but I knew Mark was trying to be kind and that he was probably right. I forced a weak smile and passed the baby to him.

"Thank you," I said.

I was still under contract to Nike, and they hadn't let go of the hope that I might return to running after I gave birth. Although I knew deep down that I never wanted to return to the world of competitive racing, I felt like I should at least try to stay in shape. I had a specialized treadmill that could allow me to run a four-minute mile in the house. After changing into my running clothes and sneakers, I climbed onto the treadmill and began to walk with the intention of getting warmed up. I lasted about two minutes before the panic and sadness overwhelmed me completely. The next thing I knew, I was curled up in a ball on the floor, face in my hands, with tears streaming down.

Why is this happening to me? I wondered. I lifted my head and looked out into the peaceful woods that surrounded our house. We lived in a beautiful home. We had each other, and now, Kylie. I didn't ever have to face the stress of racing again. There was nothing to worry about, nothing to fear. And yet, even as I told myself all of this, wishing I could feel better, nothing soothed my frayed mind. I thought of Mark upstairs with Kylie and the way he'd been watching me closely with a worried look on his face, and how I couldn't explain, even to him, what was happening to me. I thought of my parents, who were devoted to Kylie, and how any tension that had existed between me and my family because of my running had melted away, now that they could involve themselves in her care, which Mark and I were happy for them to do. I even became closer to my sisters, who had so badly wanted me to have a baby who would grow up with their own children that my sister Carrie had even offered to carry a child for me if we'd wanted to start a family while I was still competing. Our little angel had not only brought great happiness to Mark and me, but she had also brought my family back to me. I didn't want to admit how weak and vulnerable I was feeling, especially at what was supposed to be such a happy moment for us. I just wished all my feelings away.

Weeks went by, and nothing changed. Finally, I couldn't deny it anymore. The next time I took Kylie to the doctor for her shots, my doctor smiled at me as she examined Kylie.

"How are you doing?" she asked.

I took a deep breath, knowing I had to come clean.

"Actually, I'm not doing very well," I said, trying to hold back the tears.

"Well, it's normal to experience some postpartum depression after having a baby," she said.

It was a relief to know there might be an explanation for what was wrong with me, but her words didn't seem right. I had always thought that postpartum depression was when a new mother didn't want to be around her baby, and I felt just the opposite, like being close to Kylie was the *only* thing that could make me feel better.

"Do you ever have thoughts about hurting yourself or your baby?" she asked.

"No!" I said, appalled she could even suggest such a thing.

"Good, I'm glad to hear it," she said. "Try to take care of yourself and come back in two weeks. If you feel worse before then, call me."

I nodded, grateful to gather Kylie up in my arms and carry her out of the examining room, so I could get home with her where I felt safe.

In an attempt at normalcy, I threw myself into preparations for Kylie's first Christmas. Even though she was far too little to know what was going on, it was so much fun to dress her up in cute little holiday outfits and to buy her gifts and toys. And then, on December 15, the phone rang. It was Fred, Mary's husband, calling with the news I'd secretly feared.

"I'm so sorry, Suzy, but Mary passed away," he said.

The tears were instant and thick.

"She was fighting until the end," he said. "Never wanting to die, and determined not to let the cancer get the best of her. But she couldn't beat it. She's gone."

I was crying too hard to talk and I got off the line as soon as possible, collapsing in upon myself. Mary was not only my best friend, the only person besides Mark who I could be anything close to honest with, she was also the person I most admired for her strength and confidence. When I was still so far away from having a voice of my own or standing up for myself, I could at least look at Mary and feel like there was hope for me if I could just be a little more like her. And now, she was gone forever. I'd never be able to make it up to her that I'd missed her wedding so that I could race in Switzerland. She'd never have a child of her own. She'd never get to hold Kylie. We'd never again walk or talk or run together. She was really gone.

My depression deepened. Nothing calmed me except for holding Kylie, and soon even that wasn't enough. As a well-recognized celebrity in my home state, I'd frequently been approached by people who wanted me to get involved with a charity or business, and because I'd never been able to say no, I'd often agreed to even questionable collaborations, much to Mark's frustration. That was how I'd agreed to become a real estate agent, although it wasn't a career path that had ever held a particular appeal for me. Of course, what this really meant was that Mark, who already had his real estate license, ended up running our new real estate business when I failed to have the focus and organization necessary to do so. Although the business was our own, we were essentially independent contractors under the umbrella of a larger real estate firm, and our offices and website were a part of their overall organization.

Luckily, Mark's naturally calm demeanor and good nature, as well as his law background, made him a natural for his new career path, and he was soon doing quite well at a job he liked. I also enjoyed and was good at real estate, as long as I didn't have to work too much and stayed in the role that was a natural fit for me, interacting with the easier clients and staging homes and getting them ready for market.

That spring, another opportunity came my way that seemed like it might contain a solution that would smooth things over at home and maybe even lift me out of my depression. I was approached about going to work for Badger Sports Properties, an agency that sold advertising for the University of Wisconsin Athletic Department. It was a great job with amazing benefits we did not have from the real estate job, and given my passionate relationship with my old alma mater, it seemed like a natural fit. I love sports, especially University of Wisconsin sports. Mark was all for me taking the position. I wanted to be as excited as he was, but that old doubt and worry crept in, as it would be something new, without him there to hold my hand, and I felt inadequately prepared. Deep inside, I knew I was already hanging on by a very thin thread and that this job, with demands for meeting sales levels, was the last thing that would help me. I felt, though, that I owed it to Mark to try, as the income would be steady, rather than the uncertain income we earned from real estate. I thought I had to take the job. As my start date approached, a rising dread lapped at my insides, almost as bad as my pre-race anxiety. By the morning of my first day, I could barely climb out of bed, and when I finally forced myself to get ready, I started to cry.

Mark came into the room, already showered and dressed, Kylie in his arms. Since our real estate business was just in its infancy, he was able to stay home with Kylie while I was at work, and we had childcare lined up for when he needed to go to an appointment.

"Mark, I can't go," I said through tears, desperate to convince him.

"You're just overreacting," he said, taken aback by my sudden reluctance regarding a job I'd previously seemed to be excited about.

I was nearly hysterical by this point, but I forced myself to get on with it, the way I always did.

I had been right to be nervous about my new job, which I immediately hated, even though I tried to pretend to others—including Mark—that I liked it. I loved landing new clients. That part, at least, was fun. All I had to do was talk to people, mostly men, which was easy for me, and it seemed like everyone I reached out to was thrilled to take my call and schedule a meeting with me. But I noticed my clients weren't necessarily just interested in buying the advertising packages I was offering. Instead, most wanted to show me off, introduce me to their associates, and say that they had gone to lunch with three-time Olympian Suzy Favor Hamilton. Or they asked me to make an appearance at their daughter's school, or some other favor that had nothing to do with my job, which I felt like I had to do to keep them happy and perhaps close a sale. Even so, it was better than being in the office, where I worked with all men who I felt treated me like a blond bimbo and a boss who seemed to be constantly looking over my shoulder and second-guessing my work. Of course, looking back, I realize that my coworkers could probably see what I couldn't at the time: that largely because of my name, I had landed a job I was woefully underqualified for. Although I was making sales, it was impossible to earn a higher salary, and I felt trapped in a no-win situation. I started to wonder what I was doing, staying at a job I hated that took me away from my most important role in life, as a mother, but I felt powerless to push for what I needed. In addition to my ad sales job, I was helping Mark with our real estate business in the evenings and on weekends. And what had started as a few motivational speeches here and there was blossoming into a busy motivational-speaking career that often required me to travel. I was increasingly exhausted and frayed, but I just did my best to hold on to all of the strands.

◆ ◆ ◆

Information is power, and this is especially true when it comes to mental illness. Unfortunately, we are still far behind where we need to be as a culture. Take the link between postpartum depression and bipolar disorder, which doctors are just beginning to understand. As recent studies have shown, all women run the risk of developing bipolar disorder in the wake of childbirth because of the hormone plunge that occurs at this time. And women with a history of depression, or a family history of depression, are even more likely to develop bipolar disorder. Unfortunately, many of the extreme emotions surrounding childbirth, from elation to the irritability that comes with sleep deprivation, seem normal, and so they are not properly evaluated as symptoms of bipolar disorder. And because of the lingering stigma surrounding mental illness, women are not always as open about the history of mental illness in their family tree as they should be. In my own case, with my family history of bipolar disorder, I should have been flagged as at-risk for becoming bipolar after I gave birth. But I was too conditioned to keep my family's secret, and too enraptured by the experience of being a new mom to think about saying anything to my doctor. And even when symptoms began to emerge, neither Mark nor I thought bipolar disorder might be a factor. We just didn't know what we were up against. Hopefully my story will help other new mothers to get the help they need sooner, without the dangers of misdiagnosis and mistreatment, and without any feelings of shame.

Chapter 7

A DIAGNOSIS

After eight months of this increasingly tenuous balancing act, I was trying to sneak into the office, late again, when my boss called me into his office.

"What time is it, Suzy?" he asked, as if I were a child.

I hated being patronized like this, and my adrenaline spiked with anger, but there was no way I was going to talk back. I just kept my head down, cheeks blazing.

"Ten o'clock," I said.

"And what time are you supposed to be here?" he asked.

"Nine o'clock," I said.

"This seems to be a real problem for you," he said. "And I can't help but think you're overextended. I know you've been doing a lot of speaking on the side, and I'm afraid you're going to have to choose between this job or being a motivational speaker."

Instead of being upset by this ultimatum, I felt my spirits lighten immediately. Here it was: the escape I'd been so desperate for but unsure how to make happen.

"I quit," I said, my mood soaring for the first time in months.

"Excuse me?" my boss said, clearly not expecting this response.

"You asked me to choose, and I just did," I said. "I quit."

As I walked back to my desk and started clearing out my personal belongings, I was practically floating. For once, I didn't care what the other men in the office were thinking. I never had to come back there again, and I couldn't have been happier. I just had to make sure Mark was on board.

"What do you mean you quit your job?" he asked that night. "You didn't think to talk to me about it first?"

"He asked me to choose, and so I did," I said, my mood sinking under his displeasure, hating to make anyone unhappy, especially Mark. "I hated that job. I'm so happy I never have to go back there again. I wasn't meant to sit at a desk."

"Okay, Suzy." Mark sighed. "It will all work out. We'll be fine."

I started selling real estate with Mark again. On the one hand, we were a natural duo—my celebrity and bubbly personality bringing in clients, Mark's business sense and negotiation tactics sealing the deals—and we rose to the top of our agency. But the busier we became, the more pressure I felt, and even with the fifty to sixty hours a week I was soon putting in, it felt like I was never doing enough. Mark was working even more, which meant Kylie was often with her babysitter, and when I was home an increasing share of our parental duties was falling to me, from meals to bedtime. I was quickly miserable again. I was working more than I had at my last job, and I hated not seeing Kylie and hated how swamped I felt. I saw the business as hurting our marriage, and Mark was disappointed by my displeasure. I had always told him that after my running career it would be his time, and now I wasn't always holding up my end of the bargain. Tensions between Mark and me simmered, even though I could tell he was trying to be gentle. Still, I felt he was requesting too much of me. When overwhelmed, which was all of the time, I made mistakes and didn't come through on my obligations. Mark tried to cover for me, but he did sometimes call me on my shortcomings, and when he did, I was hypersensitive. It was a clear case where a husband and wife shouldn't have been working together, but we couldn't see it at the time because we'd always done everything together. I hated how no one seemed to care what I wanted, and especially hated how I felt so powerless to do anything about any of this. I couldn't bring myself to speak up and tell Mark I was unhappy and needed a change.

Over the next year and a half, I did my best to hold on, but the situation got worse and worse. By March of 2007, I was holding it together, barely, as long as Mark was home, but as soon as he went off to the office in the morning, I fell apart. My mind raced, my anxiety spiked, and I couldn't slow down. I rocked myself, back and forth, back and forth, unable to stop the motion once it started, soothed slightly by the repetition, but still not feeling good. Everything overwhelmed me, even the smallest details of life. I was in our bedroom, sitting on the bed, rocking, when our two dogs started barking at the front of the house. Rage ripped through me. *I can't handle this*, I thought, tears pressing out of my eyes. *Why won't they stop?* I rocked harder, trying to calm myself. *I can't handle this state I'm in*, I thought. *I have this baby. I have this job. It's all too much. I hate real estate. I don't get along with my husband. I just want it all to end.*

One of the few things that brought me any relief was to masturbate, and when Mark wasn't around, I would do it constantly, compulsively, unable to stop myself from my urge, instantly agitated as soon as I was done, and filled with a need to do it again. The phone rang as I started. It was Mark.

"Suzy, you were supposed to be at the open house an hour ago."

"I'm sorry, Mark."

"I can't keep covering for you," he said.

"I know. I'm sorry. I'm on my way."

Driving home from an appointment with a client that night, all the darkness I'd been feeling crested to the point where I couldn't bear it anymore. I gripped my steering wheel and prepared myself to drive my car off the road and into a tree. As I followed the windy country road through the dark stands of large oaks, my headlights glided over miles of empty asphalt, not another car in sight. I didn't want to hurt anybody else, but I didn't have to worry as long as no other cars approached. A plan formed in my mind as I accelerated faster and faster, gripping the wheel tighter and tighter. My mind raced along the road I knew so well, picturing the landscape I was about to approach. It would be so easy. *I just need to get my car up to a hundred miles an hour and then hit that patch of trees that's right around the corner, or take that next corner as hard as I can and see if I can hit that barn that's just beyond.* I was just at the point of no return, pressing the gas pedal down hard, ready to wrench the wheel to the side and veer off the road, when an even worse thought rose up from amid the chaos in my mind: *What if it doesn't work? I can't be in a hospital bed for the rest of my life. Maybe I should jump off a building like my brother did. That would be instantaneous. There would be no room for error.*

As I drove, I was getting closer and closer to home, where my sweet baby girl was waiting for me. Her face kept rising up in my mind, pressing back the dark thoughts and reminding me that I had something so much more important than me to live for now.

You can't leave your baby. What's her life going to be like without you? You have to remember the people in your life who love you. You have to remember Kylie. You have to stay alive for her.

I was exhausted and wrung out by the time I drove up our driveway and parked in front of the house. I sat there for a long moment, my fingers still gripping the steering wheel, terrified by how close I'd come to ending it all. I was in a fog that whole night, my mind still partly back on the dark roadway, consumed by my dark thoughts, which I couldn't quite shake. Mark and I were up in the loft of our house after Kylie had gone to bed for the night when he had to ask me the same question twice before I was able to focus on him enough to answer.

"What is with you, Suzy?" he said.

I was so tired, I couldn't think clearly anymore. We were always stressed around each other, always short with each other. I always seemed to forget what he needed from me, and then when he asked me about whatever it was I'd forgotten, I got mad at him for bringing it up. I was angry that I had to do this job I hated. My mind couldn't seem to hold a thought, and I was frustrated with how bad that felt—and what our marriage had become. I wanted to push him back as hard as I could so he'd finally leave me alone.

"Well, I almost killed myself tonight," I said.

The air in the room grew very still and we both just stared at each other. I hadn't been planning to tell him, ever. It just kind of slipped out of me. But as soon as I said it, I was glad I had. I knew I didn't want to die, even if I didn't know how to get better.

Mark immediately softened. The anger went right out of him and he walked across the bedroom and hugged me.

"Immediately, this second, I want you to call the doctor," he said. "And if you don't call, I'm calling for you."

I didn't want to call. I was scared of admitting how bad things had gotten, just like I was scared of everything else. But he had his arms around me, and his support gave me courage. I went downstairs and picked up the phone. And then, when the receptionist answered, I nearly hung up. It hadn't occurred to me that I would have to tell a complete stranger what I was feeling.

"I need to see the doctor right away," I said, finally.

"I'm sorry, but you can't see her for three months," the receptionist said. "She's booked."

I wondered if I should hang up the phone, but Mark came up behind me just then, and I knew I didn't have a choice, because he was going to act if I didn't. I knew I had to tell her, but I didn't want to say the words out loud. Everyone in Madison knew me. What if they found out I'd nearly killed myself? What would they think? "I almost killed myself tonight, and I need to see a doctor right away," I said.

"We need you to come in first thing in the morning," she said. "Are you okay right now? Are you going to do anything that means we need to get you to the hospital?"

I looked over at Mark, who was watching me closely.

"My husband's here," I said. "I'm going to be okay."

But I didn't feel like I was going to be okay. When I got to the office in the morning, I could barely look at the nurse who filled out my chart.

"So what's the reason for your visit today?" she asked.

I was filled with panic. I clasped my hands together in my lap and focused on not running out of the office right that minute.

"I'm not feeling good," I said.

When my doctor walked through the door and smiled at me, I immediately started weeping uncontrollably. She sat down really close to me and made me look at her.

"I just want you to know, it's going to be okay," she said. "We're going to help you and you're going to be okay."

Instead of feeling reassured, I was skeptical. Everything

felt so hopeless. *Are you serious?* I thought. *How in the world do you know I'm going to be okay?*

At the same time, if a medical professional was telling me she was going to help me, then that meant that somebody was acknowledging that something was wrong with me, and after so many months of wading through the sludge of my depression, it was a relief. I knew I had to be completely honest about what I was experiencing if I was ever going to get better.

"I was thinking about killing myself last night," I said.

"I think there's a good chance you have depression," she said. "I want to get you on medication right away. I'm prescribing you Prozac, and I'm calling it in, immediately, to the pharmacy. I want you to go pick that up as soon as you leave here."

I could feel Mark keeping an eye on me after this episode. Just like I'd felt at the doctor's office, it was a relief to finally have everything out in the open and a feeling that some relief might actually come. And slowly, it did. Not right away, but once the Prozac started to take effect, it made all the difference. The fog I'd been living in lifted and I actually had moments when I felt happy, seeing the sunshine out our window in the morning, catching my daughter's smile. We decided to move back to Madison to shorten the commute, and so Kylie would be closer to school and friends as she grew older. I threw myself into the excitement of the move, setting up a new house, and exploring a new neighborhood.

My doctor also referred me to a psychologist the day after our initial appointment, and that did not go quite so smoothly. He decided that I needed to have a group therapy session with everyone in my family—Mark, my parents, my sisters, and my brothers-in-law. I knew this was a bad idea, and I never allowed it to happen. As soon as the session was over, I called my medical doctor and had her refer me to another psychologist, who I saw twice a week for a year.

I still felt that my sisters resented me for the way running had singled me out from them and taken me away from our family, for being ungrateful for all my parents had done for me, and for pushing them away and acting like I was better than them. I thought my parents had never really forgiven me for moving away to California. With my brother's suicide still casting a shadow over all of us, we were still very raw around each other. And even subjects that could have brought us together didn't. Around that time, I learned that I was not the only member of my family who had been on Prozac, and I thought it might help them to understand where I was coming from if they knew I was being treated for depression, too. One day, toward the end of a family visit, we were all in my mother and father's kitchen. As I prepared to leave, Kris mentioned a family friend who had thought about killing himself.

"Yeah, I thought about killing myself, too," I said as casually as possible, putting on my coat. "And I take Prozac now."

Kris looked at my mother but neither said anything. Even after what had happened to Dan, silence was still the way in our family. I hadn't really been expecting a reaction, but their lack of response stung a little. I went to find Mark and Kylie so we could go home, where I felt safe to be myself.

After a year of therapy and medication, I started to feel like I was all better, like I was cured. It seemed like my therapist and I had run out of things to talk about, and she released me from treatment. In fact, I felt so good that about four years after I'd started taking it, I decided to go off my Prozac, too. I didn't like the side effects; I'd gained weight and felt sluggish and lethargic. After being an incredibly active, fit professional athlete my whole life, I was embarrassed by the way I looked now. I hated it.

At first, life without Prozac was fine. We'd settled into a life we liked in Madison, and I was busy with Kylie and the work I continued to do with Mark at the real estate agency. Although my state of mind was much better than it had been, my job was still a source of stress. I couldn't seem to do anything right, and I was constantly making mistakes, missing appointments, and embarrassing Mark, or that's how I felt. I was convinced he was always unhappy with me, and yet I couldn't tell him how overwhelmed I felt or how much I wanted to stop doing real estate.

Within three or four months, my depression crept back in, my mind once again spinning out of control. It started with a dark thought I couldn't shut off about hurting myself. The thought went away, then came back again. If someone had told me to smile, I couldn't have done it. Eddies of anxiety whirled through me. I couldn't sit still. But I couldn't seem to finish anything I started. I paced. I rocked. I started masturbating obsessively again. Everything was back, with a vengeance. I needed help, again.

I called my doctor for an appointment, and again, I was told it would be nearly three months before I could get in. Well, this time, I wasn't really on the verge of killing myself, and so I didn't want to make a fuss. I figured if I could just go back on Prozac, everything would be fine. I found a different doctor who could see me that week. When I went in for our appointment, I explained what was going on with me.

"I've had depression, and I went off my medication," I said. "Somebody told me that if you go off the drug you were on and then try to take it again, it won't have the same effect."

"Well, let's have you take Zoloft, then," she said. "It's good for depression."

"Okay, great," I said.

I was relieved to think it could be as easy as that, and in a couple months, I'd be feeling better again, just like I had after taking the Prozac. And it's true, it only took about six weeks for the drugs to kick in and start changing things. Only, this time, everything didn't go back to normal. Just as with Prozac, in a matter of a few weeks, I could feel the Zoloft working. I didn't feel depressed anymore. In fact, I felt great. I definitely didn't want to die. I wanted to live with a capital *L*. I wanted to live like I had never lived before. I wanted to run half marathons. I wanted to experiment, try new things, and have adventures far beyond our ordinary life in Madison, which now seemed too predictable and boring.

I suddenly had more energy than I could remember having for ages, and it felt amazing, especially after the heavy dullness of the depression. I couldn't wait to get up in the morning, and I made plans for all the things I wanted to do every day, zipping from one task to another, while already looking ahead to whatever I would do next.

Since officially retiring from competitive running following

Kylie's birth in 2005, I had been able to build a successful side career as a motivational speaker. I had soon started going far beyond the talks about self-esteem and positive visualization given by most athletes and begun talking candidly about my depression and my brother's death. Even on my darkest days, when it was hard for me to get out of bed, speaking came naturally to me, and I never felt nervous before an appearance. It felt so good to finally open up about a topic my family had never let me discuss, and to find that I had the power to help people, who came up to me after my events to confess their own problems and tell me how much strength and hope they'd drawn from my words. And now that the Zoloft had kicked in, I was being asked to make more and more appearances, which I loved, because all of my energy and enthusiasm seemed to be focused in the best possible way when I was speaking to a crowd.

I kept hearing that people liked the pep and positivity I brought to my talks, which usually found me getting the whole crowd up and dancing at the end. I wanted the people in the audience to feel as happy and free as I did, and for me, that meant being in motion, always in motion. I loved looking out over a sea of faces and seeing their expressions transform from reluctant embarrassment, when I first told them to get up and dance, into the kind of unselfconscious happiness I felt. That, to me, was a successful event. I wanted to do as many of them as I could. The only damper to my happiness about my public speaking success was my family's reaction. Wisconsin was a small state, and it didn't take long for word to reach them that I'd begun talking about Dan publicly. My mother was so upset that she called an all-family meeting. While I knew she just wanted her family to be as close as possible, it felt like she was asking my sisters to gang up on me and take her side, and I left the conversation feeling more misunderstood and distant from my family than I ever had before.

Overall, I was excited about life again. As Mark and I began planning a special way to celebrate our twentieth wedding anniversary on May 25, 2011, I was full of ideas for fun adventures we could have together. We both knew we needed to do something big, not only because we were approaching such a milestone in our relationship, but also because conflict at work and at home had been rising for years. Over the course of the five years we had worked together, as tensions escalated, it had gotten to the point where Mark often chose to spend long hours away from home, sometimes staying at the gym after work until past midnight. And when we were in the same place at the same time, it was common for us to fight. Although we were careful to always wait until Kylie was asleep or out of the house, sometimes our emotions got the best of us, and we even had a huge argument in front of Mark's father not long before our anniversary. Once again, I had messed up something Mark had asked me to do for a real estate transaction, but this time it was really serious, or so Mark said. Even though his dad was standing right there, we lit into each other, my hypersensitivity instantly touched off by any hint of criticism from him.

"Suzy, we could get sued," Mark said angrily.

"Come on, Mark," I said. "In the scheme of life, is it that big a deal?"

"Oh, it matters," Mark said. "It matters a lot. We could get sued for a hundred thousand dollars. When something comes in, pass it to me from now on, okay? I won't screw it up."

"Oh, come on, Mark," I said.

"No, seriously, Suzy, I keep telling you that you need to learn this shit, but you won't. Are you just lazy, or what?"

"I have a learning disability," I shouted. "You know that. Give me a break."

Mark didn't believe I was doing all I could for our business, but that being said, he didn't like being mad at me any more than I liked being mad at him. His solution was to take on more of the work himself. If we weren't working together, we couldn't argue. We began to grow distant from each other, and I blamed the job, never my behavior.

By this point, I was fighting back tears. I hated when he talked to me like this. I did try, but I couldn't focus. Simply passing the real estate exam had been difficult for me, and I'd had to use all of the four hours allotted.

But even with these tensions, we'd been married for a long time, and many of those years had been extremely happy. I'd always thought I had the best marriage ever, one that was unique and incredibly special. Mark had at times put my running before his own career, and he'd done so gladly because he knew I had a special talent and a rare drive, and he'd wanted to do everything in his power to help me succeed. We'd both always loved each other unconditionally, in a way we'd rarely seen among our friends. Even though I was the life of the party and a total flirt, and Mark was quieter and painstakingly meticulous in his preparations for every detail of life, we both accepted each other exactly as we were. We both got everything we needed to thrive in the relationship and knew how loved we were. Even with the recent tensions we'd experienced, we still loved each other deeply and wanted our marriage to work. When I started on the Zoloft, we were both optimistic that maybe this would lighten the mood in our relationship. And it did, at least a bit. Going into our anniversary, we were fighting less and looking forward to having the kind of romantic weekend that could reignite the spark.

Chapter 8
WHAT HAPPENS
IN VEGAS

About a month before our anniversary, on a rare night when Mark came home from his after-work trip to the gym while I was still awake, I sat up eagerly from where I'd been watching TV in bed, or at least looking in the general direction of the TV. I was too excited to really concentrate.

"I've been thinking about our anniversary," I said, leaning toward him.

Mark sat down on the edge of the bed.

"Oh yeah?"

"Let's go to Vegas," I said, already fully invested in the

plan. We'd only recently discovered Vegas, vacationing there a few times because we both really liked it.

"Works for me," Mark said, as he'd always loved Vegas.

Mark was always the one to plan everything in our life, and that's how I liked it. As he started to put together our anniversary trip, I kept thinking of all of the fun things we could do in Vegas. By the time we were five days out from our departure date, I'd come up with all of the ingredients for what I considered a perfect, wild celebration. I just had to find a way to convince him of my plan.

"When we get to Vegas, first, I think we should go skydiving," I said.

"I thought you said you'd never want to do that. Remember Dan?"

"Well, I want to do it now," I said, not feeling at all scared at the idea.

He laughed. "Okay, we could do that," he said, a bit apprehensively.

"And then," I said, pausing for drama. "I was thinking, maybe, we could hire an escort and have a threesome like we've always talked about."

Mark drew back a little and looked at me closely.

"Talking about it is one thing," he said. "Are you sure you want to actually do that?"

Although our relationship was strained now, we'd had a long and loving marriage with an adventurous sex life. We'd tried everything over the years, from sex toys to the Mile High Club, and we had talked about the possibility of having a threesome on several different occasions, even though we'd never acted on any of these conversations. Mark knew I'd always had some attraction to women, although I'd never been with anyone but him. Although I'd grown up in a conservative town, I'd traveled the world from a young age and been involved in women's sports, where it wasn't at all uncommon to be around gay athletes. But then I'd met Mark and fallen deeply in love with him. From that time on, I'd never wanted to be with anyone but him. But I had wanted to have a threesome since we were in college, and over the years, we'd both wondered if this could be a good, safe way for me to explore my sexuality without putting a strain on our marriage. Now, I had confidence and clarity. I knew I wanted a threesome, and I was ready to make it happen.

"Come on, it'll be fun," I said.

"Yeah . . . okay," he said, grinning at me, like most men would. "It will be fun."

Mark had set up the whole trip, booking us a nice suite at THEhotel at Mandalay Bay and a dinner reservation for the night of our anniversary. Now he started planning our skydiving adventure, and finally, finding a website for one of the high-end escort services. The next time we were home together, he pulled up some pictures on his computer and showed them to me.

"What do you think?" he asked, pointing to several girls we might choose from.

"She's pretty," I said, pointing to a brunette named Pearl, who looked like a nice, sweet girl who could have easily been a schoolteacher from Wisconsin.

"I thought you might like her," he said. "Pearl it is."

I looked at her picture more closely, feeling a sizzle of excitement and arousal inside of me. Were we really going to do this? Yes, we were really going to do this. I couldn't even imagine, really, what it would be like. But I had a feeling I'd enjoy it. And it seemed so easy. Maybe it was naïve of us, looking back, but we actually thought hiring an escort was completely legal. As far as we were concerned, we'd be paying Pearl for her companionship, and anything else that might happen while she was in our hotel room was just a little fun between friends. In fact, if anything, it seemed like the service was more worried about us than we were about them. When Mark called to set up the appointment with Pearl, they told him that they'd need to run a background check on him, and they asked him to provide his work number, so they could call and verify that he was who he said he was. Obviously, Mark was a little uncomfortable with this, but the woman he spoke with came across as very intelligent and professional and she put him at ease by reassuring him that she could pose as whoever he wanted her to, and she did, pretending to be a representative from Wells Fargo when she made the call. Once we were cleared, the service called back to let us know our plan was a go. She asked us questions about what we wanted for our time with Pearl, including how we preferred her to be dressed. Mark was still nervous about the whole endeavor, especially because she would be coming to our hotel room. He asked that she be dressed normally, in everyday clothes, so she'd blend in. Me, I wasn't worried about anything. I was just very, very excited.

BY THE TIME WE LANDED in Las Vegas, I was extra amped up, even for me. I felt like I was about to leap out of my skin, to the point where I could hardly sit still. In fact, the next day, when we found ourselves running late to catch the limo at another Vegas hotel that was going to take us to the skydiving location, and facing a snarl of impenetrable Vegas Strip traffic, I knew just what to do. As Mark and I stepped out of the air-conditioned oasis of our hotel into the bright dry heat of the Strip, he shook his head.

"Suzy, we're not going to make it," he said. "Let's just skip the skydiving. We can hang out by the pool until it's time for our appointment."

But I wanted to go skydiving, so skydiving we would go. I felt the old, familiar uptick of adrenaline, as if my veins were buzzing with electricity.

"Don't worry, I've got it," I said.

"What are you doing?" he asked, laughing.

Just like that, I took off, sprinting, and Mark had no choice but to fall into step alongside me. He was in the habit of working out regularly at the gym and was in good shape, so he was able to almost keep up as I raced several blocks to the hotel where we were supposed to meet our limo, getting us there just in the nick of time. I did stop short, however, when I saw the limo, which was not exactly part of the luxury Vegas experience we'd been expecting. It was an old black beater, and part of the back tail fin looked ready to fall off. But the driver was already getting out of the car and rushing over to open the door for us. Mark and I looked at each other and shrugged. I climbed into the backseat and Mark piled in after me. A young couple, along with the woman's father, was already seated inside, and we made small talk as we settled in for the drive. They were scheduled to do their jump right after us, and then we would all ride back to the Strip in the limo together.

The airstrip from which we'd make our skydiving ascent was about thirty minutes away. I was beside myself with excitement as we pulled up at the airfield, and there was no time for second thoughts anyhow. We were doing a tandem jump, which meant we'd each have an instructor strapped onto our backs, and as we approached the two men we'd be jumping with, they hurried us into our suits without taking more than a minute to give us the lesson and instructions we'd been expecting. Right away, it was go time. While the people we'd arrived with awaited their turn, we walked toward a gorgeous, brand-new plane, the bright afternoon sunlight glinting off the high sheen of its polish. Now *this* was more what we'd been expecting. Mark turned and smiled at me, finally looking a little more relaxed.

And then the men walked us right past the shiny new plane to a junky piece of shit with a missing door that looked about as structurally sound as the limo that had delivered us. Mark went back to looking nervous, but I just wanted to laugh even harder. I knew Mark was the kind of methodical planner who had researched every single detail of our skydive, making sure we chose a top-notch company that would keep us safe and give us the best experience possible. And, just like always, his meticulousness allowed me to be the one who didn't think about the details and just enjoyed the experience. This was true now more than ever.

There was one other man in the plane with us, who had told us on the way up that he was working toward a certain number of jumps. As soon as we were one mile up in the air, he smiled at us, moved toward the open doorway of the plane, and, just like that, disappeared into the sky. *Wow, he fell really fast,* I thought, looking over at Mark. His face was white. Usually I was the anxious one and he was my rock. Not today.

It took another ten or fifteen minutes for us to reach our jumping elevation. As we climbed higher into the sky, Mark looked more and more unnerved, getting a little pale in the face. After receiving a signal from his jump partner, Mark was suddenly sitting at the opening, silhouetted against the bright blue sky, and then he was gone, too, before I had time to really adjust to what was happening or how I felt about it. My stomach dipped. *Wow, maybe I've been taking this all a little too casually. I didn't even say good-bye. I wonder if he's all right.*

In a flash it was my turn, and I was being moved toward the door. The next thing I knew, I was falling down through the air. But inside I was rising up and soaring so high it was like the most powerful rush possible. There was a camera strapped onto us that shot video of me as I fell through the air. I talked to Kylie the entire time. "Oh my god, Kylie, you should do this with me someday. I will do this with you. Oh my god, this is incredible. You have to try this someday, Kylie."

Watching the distant world below us, I could see what seemed like all of Nevada, the desert stretching out in subtle variations of brown and red, all the way to Lake Mead, thirty miles outside of Las Vegas. It was spectacular. I *felt* spectacular. *Everything* was spectacular. This was the best day of my life. I whooped with pure joy.

After drifting down for several minutes, we landed in the desert, where Mark and his instructor waited for us. My instructor disconnected himself from my back and I turned around and gave him the biggest hug.

"Oh my god, you're so amazing," I said to him, reluctantly letting him go.

Standing close, I leaned in toward him flirtatiously.

"Thank you!" I continued. "Thank you! That was so fucking amazing."

I loved him. I loved Mark. I loved *everyone*. I loved the whole world. I was practically jumping up and down.

"Well, you're fantastic," my jump partner said with a laugh. "I wish I could jump with you every time."

"Can we go again?" I asked, ready to do just that.

Mark laughed and shook his head, like I was a little kid getting off of a roller coaster asking for another ride. He was used to my flirting and didn't take it seriously, especially on this day that was all about celebrating us and how far we'd come.

"We've got to get back," Mark said. "We have to rush as it is."

I was disappointed, but only for an instant, when I thought about what would come next. I could hardly wait for the others to finish their jump so we could make our return trip. When we were finally en route, the car suddenly came to an abrupt stop on the side of the highway. As we watched in bewilderment, the driver ran by our window to the trunk of the car. Mark opened the door and a blast of hot desert air hit us full on as he climbed out to investigate. Never wanting to miss out on a possible adventure, I was close behind him. As we came around the back of the car, the driver was bent down, tearing off a piece of duct tape, which he was using to secure a piece of the wobbly tail fin to the rest of the car.

"You've got to be kidding me," Mark said, pacing away a few feet.

I laughed. I was thoroughly enjoying myself.

"Oh yeah, hey," the driver said, looking up at us sheepishly. "I am so sorry about that. Don't worry, though, everything is taken care of now, and we'll get you back on the road right away. We'll be back on the Strip in fifteen minutes. Tops."

I felt a wild giggle rising inside of me, like the need to sneeze, but I managed to push it back. All the mishaps only made it better. Now *this* was an adventure.

"Hey, let me make it up to you," the driver said.

Again, Mark and I looked at each other, this time with curiosity, as the driver reached into the back of the car. When he reappeared, he was holding two cans of Coors Light, and he extended one to each of us. "Here, it's on me," he said.

Mark and I both looked down at the cans in our hands and looked back at each other. Again, not exactly the luxe Vegas experience we'd planned for our anniversary. But it *was* pretty funny. We both started to laugh as we climbed back into the limousine. We each opened our cans and knocked them together with a dull clunk.

"Cheers," Mark said.

"Cheers," I replied.

"Classy," he said.

We both laughed harder and drank our beers.

I was already giddy with endorphins from skydiving when we got back to our hotel room just after six o'clock. The escort was due at seven. I pulled on a special bra-and-panty set I'd brought along for the occasion and then slid into a light blue sundress. It was short enough to show off my legs and looked good against my skin, which was tan from spending the previous day by Mandalay Bay's huge pool, although I'd barely been able to make myself stretch out on one of the chaise longues, and I'd been far from relaxed. I'd felt giddy and sparkly with anticipation all day—but now my mood was slightly shadowed with nerves. I kept wondering what it would be like when she got there. I suspected the girl in the photo would not be the girl who showed up at the door. I was expecting a stereotypical prostitute, unable to hide how worn out she was, even with her big hair, heavy makeup, and skimpy clothes. I didn't know if I would even be attracted to her, and if I was, if I'd like how that would feel.

"Are you okay?" Mark asked, looking over at me as he buttoned his dress shirt, which he was wearing with blue jeans. He looked handsome and casual. Nervous or not, this was exactly the kind of adventure I'd been craving. I looked in the mirror and shook out my light brown hair, which hung down loose over my shoulders.

"Yeah, I feel great," I said, partly as a pep talk. "I'm really excited."

"Do you want a little vodka to relax?" Mark asked, crossing to the bar.

"Sure," I said.

We sat and sipped our vodkas together, unable to keep our eyes from drifting from our view of the Strip, where the sun was setting and the lights were pulsing even brighter against the darkening sky, to the clock by the bed. At exactly 7 P.M., not a minute later, there was a knock on our door. My nerves pinched and fluttered as I jumped up to let Pearl in, excited to see what she looked like and to experience whatever would happen next. I opened the door slowly, and there she was.

Pearl strolled in looking happy and relaxed, like she'd known us forever. I was immediately impressed and already a little turned on. She was a beautiful girl, and she had a golden glow about her, as if she had just climbed out of the swimming pool at our hotel, sliding into her cute jean shorts to come up and see us. Her shoulder-length caramel-colored hair was streaked with blond, and although she was wearing makeup, it wasn't too heavy. She looked fresh-faced and cute, just like she had in her photo on the Internet.

"Feel free to take a seat," Mark said, gesturing her toward one of the seats in the lounge area of our suite.

She looked at me and smiled, waiting to see where I would sit. When I slid onto the sleek cream-colored couch with its view of the Vegas Strip, she slowly and very deliberately sat down close to me, leaning her body slightly in toward mine.

"Is this your first time in Vegas?" she asked, her tone flirtatiously letting us know there was more to that question.

This is going to be fun, I thought, my high ratcheting up even higher.

"We love Vegas," I said. "We don't get out here as much as we'd like to because we live in Wisconsin, but we've been here a few times now."

"And what's the occasion for this trip?" she asked.

"It's our twentieth wedding anniversary," Mark said, approaching us with a drink for Pearl and a fresh drink for me.

"No," she teased. "It can't possibly be. You don't look old enough."

Mark and I both laughed, but he looked a little nervous beneath his cool demeanor.

"We met in college," he said.

My nerves evaporated. I felt totally comfortable with what was happening, and after a few more pleasantries, I really liked this woman. She was bright and smart and could carry on a great conversation. If we'd met in our regular lives, we could have been friends.

"Do you love living in Vegas?" I asked.

"It's the best," she said. "My other job is as a hostess at one of the big casinos. I get to meet all sorts of people from around the world. It's pretty amazing. I mean, I get to make people's fantasies come true. What could be better? I really enjoy it."

"That does sound amazing," I said, thinking it sounded like a great life, for sure a lot better than the boring and suffocating existence that I was beginning to see as grinding me down back in Madison.

She looked at me with real warmth and gave me a knowing grin. And then, still holding my gaze with hers, she finished her drink and, slow and sexy, stood up.

"Shall we?" she asked, already walking toward the bedroom.

Mark and I looked at each other and smiled with a look that said, *this is it*. My nervousness had left me as soon as I saw how nice and normal she was, but I still wondered what was going to happen and if I would like it. Mark still seemed a little nervous, which I wasn't used to, but I could tell by his forced smile that he wanted me to be happy and enjoy myself and he'd do everything he could to help make that happen.

We both followed her into the bedroom. Without any hesitation, she stripped down to her bra and panties and climbed up onto the bed. Her smooth skin looked very tan against the crisp white bedspread and the oversized quilted headboard, and my gaze was drawn to the sparkly earring in her belly button, just like she'd worn in her photo. She gestured me over to the bed and, kneeling to be at my height, helped me to slide my dress over my head, so in an instant, I was wearing only my bra and panties. We stood close together for a long moment, and then she kissed me, like *really* kissed me.

I'd fantasized about women for the last twenty years, but I'd never kissed a woman except a peck on the cheek, and I wasn't sure what to expect. She was gentle and smooth, and she smelled good, and all of her motions were slow and deliberate. I was very aware of the feeling of her tongue in my mouth, and how soft and silky her skin was as it grazed against mine where our limbs were touching as I stood in front of her. And then she pulled me down onto the bed next to her. *I'm kissing a woman.* But now, I wasn't daydreaming in a casual, curious way. I was really doing it, really having the adventure I'd been craving. My head spun with the feeling and my body heated up.

I was very turned on and very happy. I'd long wondered what it would be like to be with a woman, and here I was having this incredible experience, and sharing it with Mark, my husband and my best friend. He stood nearby, still fully dressed, watching us. As Pearl took off my bra and started to kiss down my neck, he slowly undressed. Eventually, we had Mark join us on the bed. He clearly wanted this to be a great experience for us, and especially for me, and he was very gentle and positive. This was to be all about me.

I couldn't believe how relaxed I felt, like this was the most normal thing in the world. *Why didn't we try this sooner? Why don't people do this all the time?* As Pearl moved things along, she seemed so sweet and classy, and I genuinely felt myself connecting with her. At the same time, I felt closer to Mark than I had in a long time. As far as I was concerned, this was the perfect anniversary celebration. It felt really good.

And then, at exactly eight o'clock, Pearl got up and went into the bathroom. I could hear the shower go on and smell the soap drifting out toward us on a puff of hot steam. It seemed strange to me that she'd so abruptly finished what for me had been a life-changing experience, and jumped right up to clean herself off. But I figured that must be how it's done. I lay on the bed, floating inside my own skin, filled up with the pleasure of what had just happened and with all of the sensations and feelings it had released inside of me.

"Mark, you need to give her a huge tip," I whispered, rolling over toward him.

He raised an eyebrow at me, knowing we were already paying a thousand dollars for the hour.

"Of course," he said. "I will."

As Pearl came out of the bathroom, she was clearly in a hurry to dress and leave, but was professional and polite.

"You guys are such a wonderful couple," she said. "I hope I'll see you again."

Of course you will, I thought as I closed the door behind her.

◆ ◆ ◆

Diagnosing bipolar disorder is a very tricky thing. There's no biological or genetic test, and the average time between when a patient shows her first symptom and receives an accurate diagnosis is ten to twelve years, according to recent studies. Misdiagnosis happens all the time. In my case, there was the added complication of my competitive running, which I now believe helped to keep my own symptoms at bay for years. When I stopped running competitively to have my daughter, the combination of this change to my system and my postpartum depression kicked my bipolar disorder into high gear. Not that anyone in my life—including my doctors—knew it at the time.

Because I thought I suffered from depression, which had been successfully treated with Prozac, it made sense when I was later prescribed Zoloft for my recurring depression. Little did we know at the time that giving a bipolar person Zoloft is worse than leaving them untreated. The drug not only made my symptoms worse, but it gave Mark and me the illusion that it had knocked out my illness and everything was great now. So when my behavior became more and more extreme, it never occurred to us that there was anything wrong. At the time, I didn't just feel not depressed. I felt on top of the world. Of course I wasn't going to go see a doctor when I felt this energetic and alive. It's only now that I've been successfully diagnosed as bipolar and medicated appropriately for my condition, as well as having so many triggers removed from my life, that I can see how dangerous the combination of bipolar disorder and Zoloft were.

I think the hardest part of my recovery has been looking back at my behavior that was so destructive to my marriage, my family, and myself, and finding a way to make sense of it as the illness working through me, not something I consciously chose myself. While Mark has helped me to reach a place where I have no shame about anything I did—because that would in essence mean being ashamed of being bipolar, which I absolutely am not—it's still difficult to forgive myself for the pain I caused, because of my illness, to people I love so much. Mostly, these days, I just try to focus on gratitude. I am so incredibly grateful that I was eventually diagnosed and treated, and that my loving husband and family stuck by me through all of this, because I know how easily I could have ended up like my brother Dan or so many other casualties of the disease.

Chapter 9

EXPLORATION

J ust like that, it was over, and Mark and I were alone in our hotel room, as we'd been alone together on so many occasions over the past twenty years. Only now, everything had changed. I knew it instantly. We'd spent the day jumping out of an airplane and having a threesome, things most people would only fantasize about doing, if even that. And I wanted every day to be just like this from now on. I was on fire, filled with energy. I never wanted this day to end. All at once, I was ravenous.

"I'm starving," I said.

"Me, too," Mark said. "It's almost time for our dinner reservation."

As I got dressed and fixed my makeup, I couldn't stop looking at myself in the mirror. On the outside, I looked the same as I always had, but I had done things. I knew things. I wasn't just Suzy Favor Hamilton, the nice girl from Wisconsin who had been an Olympic runner and was now a real estate agent, wife, and mom. I was a woman who brought her fantasies to life, even if they were not the kind of things nice girls did.

As we got into the elevator, my high hadn't abated. I felt amazing.

I looked up at Mark, trying to sense how he felt and what all of this meant to him.

"Do you feel different?" I asked.

He looked down at me, his face a question.

"What do you mean?"

"Well, more confident, like you just did something most people wouldn't do."

"Sure, it was pretty awesome, but I'm not sure I feel different," he said. "I do know I'm starved as hell."

I laughed at his joke, but I felt a little disappointed, too. Maybe he didn't get it. Maybe it didn't mean the same thing for him as it did for me. That was okay, I reassured myself. I knew we'd do it again. As the elevator doors opened, releasing us into the swarming crowds of people in the hotel lobby, I couldn't stop looking at everyone I saw, wondering if they'd ever had a threesome or what the craziest thing they'd ever done in bed was, and thinking how weird it was that they couldn't tell what I had just done or how it had changed me completely, how they had no idea what they were missing out on—the best experience. I had found a new way to make myself feel good, to get the adventure I craved, and I wanted more. Mark hurried me along to the taxi that would take us to dinner at Bouchon at the Venetian, as I tried to make my point to Mark, struggling to keep up in my high heels.

"I mean it, Mark," I said. "Wasn't that incredible?"

"Of course," he said. "It was great, but maybe not quite up to my expectations."

It was amazing, I thought, trying to understand how he could have felt anything other than totally amazing.

Even as we settled into our candlelit table at Bouchon and I sipped a glass of pinot noir—my favorite—from the elegant oversized wineglass and listened to the murmur of dinner conversation around me, I couldn't relax and enjoy my dinner. Images and sensations from the day flashed through my mind in rapid-fire flashes. Next to me, Mark studied the menu and laughed off my enthusiasm about the experience. I realized I might have to make it happen on my own next time if Mark wasn't as into it as I was. And that was just fine with me. I still loved Mark deeply, and I enjoyed the rest of our night together, but something had shifted inside of me. I didn't want to be defined only by my marriage. I wanted more. And, as far as I was concerned, what I wanted wasn't in Madison anymore. It was in Las Vegas.

When we got home from our anniversary trip, life seemed flat and stale. There was nothing to look forward to now that our adventure was over, and I couldn't seem to concentrate on my regular life. Our marriage had been fairly strained going into Vegas, to the point where it sometimes felt as if we were separated. Our anniversary was supposed to rekindle our passion for each other. We'd both held out hope that we'd reconnect during our weekend away, but when we returned to the real world, the bond just wasn't there. We avoided each other as much as we could around the house, and when we did talk, we were both short with each other and usually ended up arguing about something related to work or Kylie. It got to a place where I didn't even want to answer the phone when I saw Mark's name come up on the screen.

I thought we were being torn apart by our real estate business. Mark coped with the strain by immersing himself more and more in work and our daughter. I couldn't see how hypersensitive I was, or what a nightmare it was for him to deal with my mood swings and extreme irritability. I simply wanted him to leave me alone. We faced more of the same sexless, lifeless marriage we'd had before Vegas, but now, I couldn't stand it any longer. I'd found happiness in Vegas, which had finally taken me out of my anxiety and sadness, and I wanted more sex and thrills, even if it distanced me further from Mark, who was in a very different place.

I even had trouble focusing on Kylie, who had always brought me so much happiness. It was like my mind couldn't stay still long enough to follow the simple routines of my day with her, the regular snacks and games and television programs. My imagination went back again and again to the only place where I felt happy and satisfied—Las Vegas. I thought about our threesome constantly, replaying the details in my mind until they became so familiar they lost their luster for me, and then I started thinking about what would happen the next time I went back to Vegas, about what I would do when I saw Pearl, and about things I might do with people other than Pearl. I thought about sex all the time, until it got to the point where my fantasy was more real than my real life was.

About a week after our anniversary, I was waiting up for Mark when he got home, even though it was almost midnight. When he walked into the bedroom, he seemed surprised to see me awake and alert, sitting up against the pillows.

"Mark, I've been thinking," I said. "Do you think we should go back to Vegas?"

"But we were just in Vegas," he said. "I'm not sure I can get away again."

"Well, what if I just went, then?" I said.

"Yeah, sure," Mark said. "It would probably be good for you. Get some alone time."

"You know, if you ever want to go to Vegas by yourself, I'd be okay with that," I said.

He nodded, both of us understanding that we were moving toward giving each other space within our marriage, maybe even giving each other permission to stray for the intimacy each of us was lacking and missing, as long as it was just sex and not an affair. We'd gone to Vegas on our anniversary as an attempt to reconnect and return the spark to our marriage. While we'd enjoyed our time together there, we'd come out of the experience in such different places that we'd both shifted our focus to finding ways to stay married while satisfying ourselves on our own terms, even if that meant opening up our marriage in ways not everyone would feel comfortable with.

"I'm okay with you going to Vegas alone, too," he said. "But you've got to be safe and discreet."

"Of course," I said, feeling elated by the possibility of my new freedom.

That was all the encouragement I needed. I decided to meet up with an attractive young woman I'd befriended at one of the universities where I'd been hired to speak. We'd stayed in touch and began planning a fun girls' weekend in Las Vegas. Around this time, Mark and I went further in our mutual decision to explore possibly having an open marriage, admitting that both of us would enjoy having the chance to have sex with other people—not like an affair, because we were both committed to our marriage, but sex if the opportunity presented itself. I wasn't threatened by the idea of Mark being with another woman because I knew our marriage was something special and rare, even though we had hit a rough patch, and I knew he felt the same way. As with everything else, we were completely open with each other and discussed every aspect of how we were feeling and what this step would mean for our relationship. I was all for Mark's extramarital activity because it meant that I'd get to continue exploring my own desires, too. I even hoped he would see someone else because I felt guilty about my need to seek pleasure outside our relationship; if he did so, too, it would make me feel better about my own urges. I made it clear to him that I wanted intimacy and excitement I wasn't getting from our relationship at that point, and we both gave each other the green light to seek intimacy elsewhere. We were equally comfortable with transitioning into an open marriage, and neither of us thought about divorce. We knew our marriage was in trouble, but we were both willing to do whatever it took to keep it together, even if we had to go to some unconventional lengths to do so.

When it came time for my next Vegas trip, I was thrilled that I was getting everything I wanted, especially because my new friend happened to be gay, and I hoped we might even have a little tryst while we were away. But even though we'd flirted by text before our rendezvous, from the moment I arrived, I was disappointed. I was looking for a few days of casual sex, whereas my new friend wanted a platonic relationship. We were there for different reasons. Our trip was fun, but it lacked the glamour and excitement I was craving, and it was instantly clear that we were better off as friends, which we are to this day. When Mark and I had gone to Las Vegas and had our threesome, it had been like we were part of an elite club where fantasies came true, and that's what I wanted to recapture. It hadn't happened this time around. I went back to Madison planning to return as soon as I could, laying my plan out for Mark.

"I know I was just in Vegas, but I want to go back," I said.

"Again?" Mark said. "Why?"

"Well, I was thinking, maybe I could see Pearl again?" I said. "You know I've never been with anyone but you, and I've always been curious about that side of myself. I really enjoyed that, and it would make me happy."

"Yeah, that would be okay," he said, laughing. "I know you have a crush on her."

"And . . ." I didn't know if I was asking for too much, but

honestly, I didn't know if I cared. "Maybe I could go see a male escort, too?"

He visibly flinched. Even though we'd talked about opening our marriage up, it felt different now that it was really happening. Mark found himself worrying that if I went to see a male escort, it could open things up too far, into dangerous territory.

"Why?" he asked.

"Come on, there's no harm in it," I said. "He's an escort. It's not like I'm going to have a relationship with him. It's just for fun."

Because we'd both always had fairly liberal views on sexuality, and believed there was a big difference between a committed relationship and "just sex," Mark finally nodded his head.

"Thank you, Mark," I said, filled with love and gratitude for him. Yes, I still loved my husband and believed in our marriage, but it wasn't enough to make me happy on its own anymore. Maybe, just maybe, I could have everything.

Sex and excitement were on my mind more than usual in those days, and specifically, my next sexual adventure in Vegas. Scenes from our appointment with Pearl played through my mind constantly, when I was washing the dishes, when I was driving to the grocery store, and especially when I was running, which I was back to doing as much as I could, because it gave me time alone with my increasingly elaborate fantasies. I did have the clarity to understand how lucky I was that I had a loving husband who was willing to try to make our marriage work. I knew that most other husbands would not be so open-minded. At the same time, it all seemed completely normal. It was what I wanted, so it must be okay.

Mark didn't seem upset that I'd asked him for his blessing to have sex with another person. He seemed really tired, which was how he seemed a lot of the time. Not that I was in the habit of slowing down long enough to focus too much on what he was feeling. I was on a mission, devoted to my own feelings, experiencing pleasure and getting what I wanted—and I didn't want to slow down for anything. The thought of my trip to Vegas made me so excited I could hardly sleep most nights

TWO WEEKS LATER, I WAS in Vegas again. Mark and I had left it that I would definitely see Pearl, as well as a male escort, Sebastian, from the same service. Mark had helped me book my trip, which I think at least made him feel a little better about the whole endeavor from a safety standpoint. Not that I was thinking about Mark as soon as my plane touched down in Las Vegas. Experiencing complete independence for the time I was there felt amazing. It was a welcome break I was beginning to think I might need every so often while Mark and I figured out a way to work things out down the line. I was particularly happy to be away from the real estate business, which I detested and blamed for all of our problems. I'd recently suffered some nasty verbal abuse at the hands of an unhappy client who'd lost money on the sale of his home, his poor investment. I'd hated how small and stupid I felt as I sat in that coffee shop across from this man, allowing myself to just shut up and take it, even though I wanted to do anything but. Such extreme suppression of myself felt almost as bad as it had when I'd made myself compete in the face of my worst anxiety, like I had no voice and what I wanted didn't matter. I didn't want to be that person anymore, and in Vegas, I didn't have to be. I could forget all that for the next seventy-two hours, and I would.

From the minute I arrived, I was on a mission. This was my playground, where I could be free to enjoy this new side of myself, and do whatever I wanted. Finally, I had the chance to make up for all that I had missed out on by being a nice girl my whole life. Who cared that I was in my forties?

I'd gone to Vegas with the intention to see Pearl, but when I got there I decided I wanted to see the male escort, Sebastian, first instead. It was easy enough to change my plan through the service, and I was soon anticipating my upcoming tryst. I spent a long time getting ready in front of the big mirrors in the bathroom, loving the knowledge that in a few hours Sebastian would arrive at my room. I carefully applied my makeup and straightened my hair, and then I counted out three hundred dollars in cash. As I'd learned, male escorts generally charged less than females because there wasn't as much demand for their services. I slid the money into an envelope and left it on the vanity in the bathroom, as I'd been instructed. Just at the hour we'd specified, Sebastian knocked on the door of my room and I felt a thrill of excitement and nerves. I'd chosen him over the service's other male escort because he looked the part of the gigolo, and that's what I wanted: pure fantasy. When I opened the door, there he was: six-foot-two, incredible body, beautiful black skin, his clothes hanging on him just right, in a sexy, casual way, like he'd just stepped out of a magazine.

"Hey, Suzy," he said. "How are you tonight?"

"Great," I said. "Come on in."

Just as Pearl had done, he walked in casually, like we were already lovers and he'd been waiting all day just to see me. My adrenaline was already racing and I started talking a mile a minute. In my excitement, the words just kind of poured out of me.

"Do you want a drink?" I asked. "I'm going to have vodka. Normally I drink wine. Red wine. Pinot noir is my favorite. But on special occasions I like to drink vodka and cranberry. And this seems like a special occasion, doesn't it?"

"It sure does," he said, his voice as flirtatious as mine. "I'll have whatever you're having."

Here I was, standing at the bar in a swanky hotel room in Las Vegas, mixing a drink for a gigolo, my gigolo.

"So do you live in Vegas?" I asked.

"Yeah, I moved here to play basketball in college," he said.

"Really?" I said. "I was a college athlete, too."

"Oh yeah?" he said. "You definitely have an athlete's body. What did you play?"

A little spike of reality managed to penetrate my fantasy. One of Mark's biggest concerns about my desire to step outside of our marriage was that someone might recognize me. I was still enough of a public figure, especially in Madison, that it wouldn't take much for a rumor to get started. Although I had no reason to, I already trusted this man, but I figured I should be careful.

"I was a gymnast," I said.

"Hot," he said, giving me a sexy look.

"What are you studying?" I asked.

"I'm out of school now, and I do some modeling in L.A., so I split my time between there and Vegas."

Now *that* was hot. This was *so* much more exciting than boring old Madison.

When I handed him his drink, he took a sip, and then, setting it down on the coffee table, he leaned over and kissed me. It was exciting, but in a different way than it had been with Pearl. Kissing a man other than my husband was a little strange, but the strangeness was a part of the thrill, too. And maybe the weirdest thing of all was that, just like everything else that went along with my new Vegas life, it felt totally normal, even when he quickly undressed me and led me to the bed. We were laughing and teasing each other like we'd been friends forever, and the sex was hot. Not just because I was a very sexual person, but because this was something special I was getting to do that almost no one else in the world got to do. This was something off-limits that no one would have expected from the nice girl from Wisconsin.

The hour went by even more quickly than it had with Pearl. This time, I wasn't surprised when he got up and went to take a shower. I knew it was time for him to go. I also knew that I'd be seeing him again, and soon. I liked him, and not just the way he looked. He was really smart, and even though he was masculine and sexy, he was also sweet and gentle with me, and we had fun together. Suddenly, even though I'd been looking forward to seeing Pearl again since pretty much the minute she kissed me, I decided I didn't want to see her anymore, not when I could sleep with this man instead. I'd have him on the side whenever I came to Vegas, and finally, I'd be happy.

"Can you come back later?" I asked, already formulating the plan in my mind.

"Definitely, I'd like that," he said, grinning wickedly at me.

"Do you want to know something?" I said. "You're the only man I've ever had sex with beside my husband."

"Now that's just a waste," he said. "I'm glad you decided to branch out."

We both laughed as I walked him to the door, where he kissed me, long and hot. After he left, I texted Mark to say everything was fine. I had promised to check in and let him know I was safe, but now that I was in Vegas, I didn't feel like talking to him and getting pulled out of the fantasy of the new life I was creating for myself.

It was easy to call the service and switch my appointment with Pearl the next day to one with Sebastian instead. The next evening when we saw each other, it was even more fun because I knew what to expect. When he didn't jump up and take a shower after fifty minutes, I was thrilled. He was having such a good time that he stayed for a full three hours, even though he only charged me for one. Our sex became more intense, and I particularly loved that I could direct the action, pushing the boundaries further and further, and by doing so, feed the energy inside of me. In fact, by the time he finally did get dressed and prepared to leave, I had an idea for how we could make things even more exciting. As he had the first time, he paused to kiss me good-bye just inside the door. I was still naked.

"I was thinking," I said, my voice laced with flirtation.

"And what were you thinking?" he asked, adopting my tone.

"Maybe you could come back tomorrow, and could you bring someone else with you?"

"And who would this someone else be?"

"Another guy?" I asked.

"Naughty, naughty," he said, laughing. "I think that could be arranged. Don't go through the screening service this time. Just text me and we'll work it out."

The next night, when I heard Sebastian knock on the door, I was filled with a sizzling thrill that was beginning to feel familiar to me. The more I felt it, the more I wanted it, and the more determined I became to feel it all the time. When I opened the door, Sebastian stood there, hot in perfectly baggy jeans and perfectly fitted T-shirt that showed off his chiseled body. And just behind him was his cousin, an equally cute and well-built guy.

"Hi, beautiful," Sebastian said, pausing to kiss me deeply in the doorway.

"Come on in, guys," I said.

His cousin followed him into the room. When we made eye contact, I smiled at him, but he looked away quickly, like he was a little nervous. I wasn't nervous at all. I was fully in my element. I could feel their eyes on my body, admiring me, as I went to the bar to mix drinks for everyone, talking and flirting the whole time. Things started out as they had before, with Sebastian undressing me and leading me to the bed. I was excited by how it felt to be there, naked, with these two handsome men. Sebastian kissed me and I arched my back under his body, feeling my skin awaken with the contact. And then his cousin joined in, but he wasn't gentle in the way Sebastian had been. He pushed on my hips, forcefully moving my body in the way he liked. He was big and strong, and he was being rough with me. I wasn't used to having my body used like this, and I didn't like how it felt. But he didn't stop. He was excited. They were both into it, and they hadn't noticed that I wasn't. I let the situation progress, trying to please them as I had always done for everyone around me. But as I lay pinned on the bed, having trouble breathing, feeling trapped and unhappy, I had a reaction that surprised me: I got mad.

Pushing myself up from underneath the cousin, I forced him off me.

"That's it," I said, raising my voice. "Leave."

"What? You're kidding," he said.

I stood up on the bed, completely naked.

"Get the hell out of here," I said.

He looked up at me and saw I wasn't kidding. Scurrying to get out of there as quickly as possible, he grabbed his clothes up from the floor and ran out the door, still pulling them on over his bare limbs. I looked at Sebastian. He was laughing, but in a nervous way, like he wasn't sure what I was going to do next. Watching me the whole time, he gathered his clothes and ran out, too. The room was suddenly empty, but I didn't feel any calmer. I strode over to the door, still completely naked, and threw it open, not caring who saw me as I watched them both run down the hallway toward the elevator.

Chapter 10

A WAKE-UP CALL

E ven though my threesome with Sebastian and his cousin hadn't gone the way I'd thought it would, the experience wasn't the wake-up call it should have been. Far from it. I didn't admit to myself that I'd gotten in over my head or that I should go back to my old life. The thought never occurred to me. I just wanted to find the next adventure, the next thrill. The mechanism within me that would have clicked on to trigger embarrassment, fear, or even self-protection wasn't working.

Even though I had always worked hard on my body, I'd never felt comfortable showing it off in my daily life. I was uncomfortable when attention was drawn to my figure during my college running career, and as a professional runner, because I'd always wanted to be whatever people expected me to be, and that also meant having the ideal runner's body. Although I'd always had an exhibitionist streak and felt completely comfortable being naked, I knew this wasn't in keeping with my image as a nice Wisconsin girl, and so I'd only allowed myself to indulge this side of myself in situations where it was permissible: when skinny-dipping with friends, on a topless beach in Europe, or when I was asked to model for a swimsuit calendar or appear naked in a Nike commercial. The rest of the time, I was as modest in my dress and body language as my mom and sisters. In fact, Mark had sometimes teased me about how frumpy my clothes were and bought me more flattering alternatives—a pair of Guess jeans in college, a pair of leather pants later in our marriage—but I'd always been too embarrassed to wear them. Even now that I was blossoming, I didn't feel comfortable wearing skimpy clothes. After the threesome with Sebastian and his cousin, I dressed for my night in the casino much as I would have at home, pulling on a pair of jeans and a loose blouse, then sweeping my hair back into a high ponytail, my signature when I was a runner. I almost never wore high heels, because I didn't want to damage my feet, so I pulled on a pair of strappy sandals. Feeling sexy, even if I didn't exactly look the part, I slipped into the hallway. I loved the sleek anonymity of the hotel, and of Vegas. Everything was luxurious, empty of memories or associations. No one had any idea who I was or what I was doing in town.

As I entered the bar in the heart of the Mandalay Bay casino area and glided up to the bartender, I was happy to be alone. In fact, it was a relief to be on my own, without responsibility for anyone else. I smiled and chatted with anyone around me, anyone who caught my eye. Within no time, I was sitting with two younger women I met at the bar who were drinking cocktails like water and clearly enjoying their Vegas vacation. There was a band playing on the adjacent stage area, and the three of us hit the dance floor. All I ever wanted was to go, go, go, so it felt natural to expend all of my energy out there among the flashing lights and sea of bodies.

The next thing I knew, one of the girls was up on the stage, and then the other, dancing suggestively as the band members egged them on and the male audience members watched appreciatively. They waved me up to join them, and I bounced up alongside them like it was the most natural thing in the world. I could feel all of those eyes on me now, and I loved it—loved looking out at the crowd and seeing men admire me, looking over at the musicians and seeing them want me. The drummer, in particular, was giving me the eye, and so, just like that, I opened up my blouse and flashed him, and he grinned like I'd just made his day. I wasn't trying to pick him up, but that didn't mean I couldn't have some fun. I laughed and danced harder, having the best night I'd had in a very long time. I *loved* Vegas.

When the song ended, I turned to hop down off the stage and find my next adventure. Before I could go, the drummer stopped me.

"Hey, afterward, you know, come by and see me," he said.

I paused with my hip cocked, looking him up and down, considering.

"No thanks," I said.

I was there to have fun, have sex, and explore this new side of myself. I would have slept with him if I'd wanted to, but he didn't appeal to me. My marriage was still important to me. But I craved everything it was lacking: passion, intimacy, and sex. And I would find these elements I so deeply desired elsewhere if necessary.

I stood sipping my glass of red wine, flushed and sweaty from dancing, happily surveying the scene and enjoying the kind of people watching I never got to do back home. As I slid into a banquette with my drink, I noticed a handsome middle-aged black man smiling at me from the next table, where he was seated with an older, very well-dressed white woman. He had this incredible, big, friendly smile, and I felt drawn to him immediately.

"Nice dancing up there," he said. "How's your night been?"

"Unbelievable," I said, laughing as I remembered the scene earlier in my room.

I thought I saw a shadow cross the woman's face, but when she looked over at me she forced a smile.

"Are you here alone?" he asked.

"Yes," I said, "but I'm still having an amazing time."

"Well, now you're with us," he said.

"Hello," the woman said, nodding at me.

"Nice to meet you," I said, leaning toward them and holding out my hand.

"Nice to meet *you*," he said, taking my hand. But instead of shaking it, he slid it under the table and placed it on his crotch for a long moment.

Whoa, I thought.

"You should come back to our room with us," he said.

"Sam," the woman said, leaning toward him as if she was trying to get his attention without me hearing her words. *"No."*

He was cute, and I was flattered, but I could tell she didn't want me around.

"I have to go," I said, draining the last of my wine.

"Here, I'll walk you out," he said, gesturing for me to stand first.

The woman smiled with her mouth, but her eyes were hard and angry.

As soon as we were about fifty feet away from their table, he held out his hand to me. "It was so nice to meet you," he said.

When I took his hand, I felt a piece of paper there in his palm, and when I looked at it, I saw it had a phone number written on it.

"Nice to meet you, too," I said, putting extra emphasis on the word *you*.

"So here's the deal," he said, talking quickly. "I'm an officer in the military, and that woman is a special friend who pays for me to meet her in Vegas a few times a year. I'd love to see you the next time I'm here, but you can't tell anyone."

"Sounds exciting," I said.

There was something about Sam. I could tell he was the kind of person who was very good not only at his job, but at anything else he put his mind to.

"Call me," he said.

"I'll think about it," I said.

Mark and I had a deal that I was supposed to call him to check in and let him know I was okay when I was in Vegas alone. But I put off calling him until I was at the airport, about to catch my flight home, and I knew I couldn't avoid it any longer. Still, after twenty years together, I was in the habit of telling my husband pretty much everything that happened. I didn't think about whether or not it would hurt his feelings.

"Are you okay?" Mark asked. "You never checked in."

"I texted you," I said.

"Yeah, but I couldn't tell much from that."

"Oh, Mark, it was great," I said. "I saw Sebastian, and he's really cool."

"Yeah? Good. I'm glad you're happy," he said.

"Yeah, I had a fantastic time. I definitely want to do it again."

"And how is our friend Pearl?"

"I canceled and saw Sebastian again instead," I said, unable to keep the enthusiasm out of my voice.

"Oh," Mark said, sounding ambivalent.

"He's awesome," I continued, caught up in my excitement about Sebastian, who was only the second man I'd ever had sex with and had left me with a little crush. "And we get along really well. He used to play basketball in college. We just get each other as we're both former athletes."

"But you didn't tell him you were a runner?" Mark said, sounding very concerned.

"I told him I was a gymnast. Relax, it's all going to be fine."

"You have to be careful, you know, Suzy," he said.

"Well, we're boarding, so I'll see you at home soon."

"I don't like this, Suzy," Mark said, sounding angry.

"You worry too much," I said, matching his tone.

"I don't think you have any idea how risky this is," he said. "And that wasn't what we talked about before you left."

"Mark, it'll all be fine," I said. "I have to go."

I could tell Mark was more threatened by having me see a male escort than a female, and that he was maybe even a little jealous of Sebastian. But I still planned to return and see Sebastian again. It wasn't that I wanted to hurt or alarm my husband. It was as if I'd suddenly become a teenager. I wanted what felt good and was fun, all the time.

AS SOON AS I GOT back to Wisconsin, I couldn't wait to leave again. I didn't want to have to pay for sex anymore, and maybe, now that I'd made a connection with Sam, I wouldn't have to. Of course, I needed to discuss everything with Mark. I needed to explain to him that my approach was going to change, but that I'd still be safe and not get emotionally involved. I wanted evidence to support my argument to Mark that I should return to Vegas and spend a couple days with Sam. He had given me his full name, so I googled him and found information that verified what he had told me about his high military rank. And then I waited until Mark and I had a few minutes alone. He was checking his e-mail on his phone when I sat next to him on the couch with our iPad in my hand, ready to make my case.

"So I've been thinking about going back to Vegas," I said.

"Already?" he said.

"You know that guy Sam I met?" I said. "The one I told you about?"

"Yeah," Mark said flatly.

"Well, look," I said, pointing to the website I'd pulled up in my research. "He's a high-ranking officer in the military, just like he told me, which means he has to be discreet. I don't want to pay for sex anymore, and if I go and meet him, I won't have to, but I also won't have to worry about him talking about anything that happens between us."

Mark took the iPad from me and studied the website I'd pulled up, then tabbed back to look at the other sites that had come up in my search and read them for himself.

"You have to be safe," he said. "And you have to be discreet."

"He can be trusted," I said.

"I hope you're right," Mark said, his tone ambivalent. "I have to leave in a few minutes or I'm going to be late."

As he stood, he was already checking messages again. As much as I wanted my freedom, a part of me was hurt that he didn't seem to care more. I had thought if I showed him that other men wanted me, it would make him want me again, too. I lacked the perspective in that moment to see how my actions could serve to drive a further wedge between us. All he seemed to care about was work anyhow.

Not that his reaction in any way impacted my decision to return to Vegas. I was too excited to stop myself.

A MONTH LATER, I RETURNED for my second solo trip to Vegas, with a plan to rendezvous with Sam on my first night in town. This time, I checked into the Vdara Hotel. I had quickly gotten hooked on the amenities that came with the best hotels in Vegas—upgrades to suites, room service, and spa treatments. It was all part of the fantasy life I was creating there. I was pleased to see that this time I had a gorgeous corner suite with a separate kitchen and living room, and the bedroom was sleek and very modern with a dark wood oversized headboard flanked by lamps with black-and-white-striped shades. There was an amazing view of the Strip below from everywhere in the room, but especially the bed.

Again, I took my time getting ready, thrilling at the idea that I was preparing myself for a night of hot sex with an attractive man who seemed to like me. Each time I went back to Vegas, I needed the thrill to be a little more intense than the time before. I had to do something a bit more daring. When I'd put on my makeup and pulled my hair into my usual high ponytail, I slid into my cutest jeans, blouse, and sandals. This was going to be my best night yet in Vegas.

I still had an hour to kill until it was time to meet Sam in the bar downstairs. I went into the bedroom and watched the water from the fountains outside the Bellagio leap up into the night sky. But I couldn't stand still for longer than a few moments at a time. I paced over to the bed and back, turned on the TV, and flipped through the channels, but I couldn't focus on the pictures. I explored every corner of the suite, enjoying how sleek and luxurious it was, until finally, bored, I went down to the bar early.

When Sam approached me at the bar, he strolled right up like an old lover and pulled me close to him, kissing my cheek. He was taller than I remembered, with that perfect military posture that made him look regal and powerful. And he was handsome, so handsome.

"Hey, gorgeous," he said. "It's so good to see you. Let me get you a drink."

He immediately got the bartender's attention and gestured for him to pour me another glass of wine. At home, I had started to bristle at the way Mark seemed to have to do everything for me, getting mad at myself as much as him because I so desperately wanted to be able to do something on my own for once in my life. But here in Vegas, where I felt in control of myself and my desires, I was attracted to Sam's easy confidence and how powerful it made him seem. His power was as much of an aphrodisiac as his looks, and I was already tingling with anticipation about what would happen when we went upstairs.

"Is this seat taken?" he joked, pulling out the seat next to me.

I laughed, enjoying the chance to be silly in a way I never got to be at home.

"It is now," I said.

"How was your flight?" he asked.

"Good. I couldn't wait to get here," I said.

"And I couldn't wait to see *you*," he said, giving me a meaningful look.

Again, I felt like I'd known him forever, like we were already friends. Well, friends who couldn't wait to tear each other's clothes off.

"Well, then, let's go up to my room, so you can see all of me," I said.

As soon as we stepped inside my room, he kissed me, and we both began stripping each other naked. The thrill of having such a sexy encounter with a virtual stranger, but one who was funny, kind, and clearly worshipped women, was revving me up even higher than I'd been before, and I threw myself into the encounter. Our sex was intense and extremely pleasurable, but we also kept laughing the whole time, like old friends. After a few hours, we both lay naked on the bed, exhausted and happy, drinking wine.

"Wow, you're really good at that," I said.

"I used to be a gigolo," he said.

"Used to be?" I asked. "What about that woman I met you with?"

"She's just a friend," he said. "She likes to spend time with me, so she pays my expenses to stay in Vegas a few times a year. It's just fun."

"Did you like being a gigolo?" I asked, totally fascinated by this new world.

"Getting paid to have sex?" he said. "Sounds terrible."

As soon as he left, I immediately wanted more of what I'd just had. As good as this felt, it wasn't enough. My brain was filled with sex. I lay in the tousled bed, the smell of sex in the room, and an image bloomed in my mind, a fantasy of three men having sex with me at the same time. I could see exactly how it would play out, could almost feel how good it would be to have all of those hands on me. It was the thrill of what I was doing and how removed it was from my other life and the Suzy I was supposed to be that made it all so amazing. I felt powerful and in control—once unfamiliar sensations for me, but quickly becoming second nature.

The next day, I finally looked at my phone, so I could text Sam to confirm dinner plans. Again, I had promised Mark I would check in to let him know I was okay, and when I hadn't done so the day before, he'd left a voice mail, his tone slightly irritated. Calling home just reminded me that I was a wife and mother, and that was part of what I was trying to forget.

I told myself I'd get my nails done, and then I'd call Mark later, before I went for dinner. I put off the call for as long as possible, and then, when I only had a five-minute window to talk, I paced in front of the wall of glass in my room as I dialed Mark.

"Suzy, simple rule, just check in," he said right away.

"I'm fine," I said. "I'm just having fun."

"You promised to check in," he said.

"I know, I lost track of time," I said. "How's Kylie?"

"She's good," he said. "You want to have your fun, fine. I just want to know you're okay. Humor me."

As soon as we got onto the topic of our daughter, the mood lightened at least a little bit. But he seemed just as glad to get off the phone as I did when I made my excuses and hung up just a few minutes later.

That night, I saw Sam a second time. He wined and dined me, and then we went back to his room for several hours. Before I flew home, I also had a quick tryst with a chef who picked me up when I sat down at the bar in his restaurant. The trip was turning out to be everything I'd fantasized it could be—exciting locale, luxurious accommodations, sexy play, and total freedom. That was it. My old life was over now.

Chapter 11

DOUBLE LIFE

My brain was no longer able to focus on reality. It liked fantasy so much more. I was barely there when I was in Madison. The only aspect of my home life that still made me happy was my daughter, Kylie. We continued our normal mom-daughter activities, like reading books together and going to Chicago to visit museums and attend events related to the American Girl line of dolls, plus trips to Disneyland during school breaks. Because I felt guilty about my desire to be away so much, I did my best to be Supermom when I was home, spoiling her and saying yes to anything she wanted. Mark tried to get me to stop, saying I was making the situation worse, but I couldn't help myself.

I continued to feel extremely estranged from my family. I was essentially divorced from my sisters at this point. And I avoided talking to my mom, who kept putting pressure on me to stop speaking publicly about Dan and, to some extent, mental illness. I did my best to avoid seeing all of them, or even talking to them. I wanted to escape my real life, and so I went away in my mind, replaying images of the sexy interludes I'd had, fantasizing about what would happen next time, plotting on how and when I'd get back to Vegas. This didn't feel selfish to me. I had lost control. I had no fear. I had no inhibitions. I had no regrets. I wasn't hurting Mark and Kylie because, in my mind, this new life had nothing to do with them. My Vegas life existed in a separate, secret bubble, where it was possible to finally have everything I wanted. In Vegas I was free. I could live on the edge of danger. I could say yes, not caring what anyone might think or say.

I decided I didn't want to keep juggling two sides of myself. I just wanted to keep building my fantasy life, away from responsibilities, and not care about the consequences. My concern was no longer making it easier for Mark to accept my next return trip to Vegas, but simply how soon I could get back there. I had told Mark about my time with Sam and the chef; although he clearly didn't want to know the details, I had no off switch anymore, even when I was back home in Madison. I made another trip a month later. Once again, my reality shifted. I got the chef I'd gone to bed with to buy me five hundred dollars' worth of clothing and jewelry in exchange for another night together. Now I was going to get something for the pleasure I gave, not the other way around. It was another step up the ladder, another step away from good girl.

Mark seemed to have accepted the dynamic of our lives now. With my knowledge, and even encouragement, he indicated he would eventually sleep with another woman. We both knew he had no desire to start an affair, and instead of feeling jealous, I was glad. It took the pressure off me and made me feel even more entitled to do what I wanted, which was of course to get myself back to Vegas as soon as I possibly could. Mark and I had essentially gone our separate ways. Gone were the expectations of how normal married couples behave toward each other. We both still put Kylie first, but after her, we were more focused on ourselves than on our marriage.

I spent my time thinking about how I could possibly live a double life, one that was primarily focused on Vegas. That fall, I was given a perfect opportunity. The Rock 'n' Roll Marathon asked me to take part in their next events, to be held in Las Vegas on Saturday, December 3, and Sunday, December 4, 2011. Because it was my first job for them, they offered to fly Mark out as well, so he came along.

During this time, I had enormous amounts of energy. When I wasn't engaging in my sexual fantasies, I would exercise. Sometimes it felt like I could exercise forever. Distance training had become a natural pastime for me, so I was thrilled to be approached by the Rock 'n' Roll organization. I couldn't have been happier to be amid the buzzing, flashing, sexy vibe of Las Vegas for my first appearance for the Rock 'n' Roll Marathon on the same weekend I was due to meet with Bridget, the woman who was my contact at the high-end escort screening service Mark and I had used to set up our first threesome. It had dawned on me that the best way to take my new life to the next level was to be a part of the thing that had sucked me into this in the first place. Pearl had introduced me to this world, had flipped a switch inside of me, awakening a certainty in me that I could please clients even more completely than she'd pleased me. I knew the thrill of getting something in return for sex because of the way the gifts from the chef had turned me on. Becoming a part-time escort myself made absolute sense. To me, if not my husband. Mark wasn't exactly happy about the idea, but I finally sold him on it by explaining to him that because the service did a background check on all of its clients, becoming an escort was actually the best way to ensure that no one ever found out about my double life. No more picking guys up at bars; it would be incredibly discreet and done only occasionally with men who had more to lose than I did if word got out. And as I had before, I told him I had to do this if I was going to be happy. Somehow, he agreed. Somehow, these sorts of discussions had become normal for us.

I'd been so excited when I'd reached out to Bridget before our trip to tell her I was interested in escorting. I wanted to discuss the idea of having occasional trysts, with just a couple of her highest-rolling, most discreet clients. When the time came, I felt nervous about how to act, how to dress, what questions to ask. I wanted to impress Bridget and convince her I'd be a good escort, and so I chose my outfit carefully. I was beginning to dress a little bit sexier lately, and I wore tight black leggings. But I also wanted her to think I'd be professional, so I wore a collared shirt, almost as if my bottom half was applying for a job as an escort and my top half was applying for a job at a bank. After putting on my makeup, I gave up trying to figure out what was the normal way to behave and rushed out to meet her. When I arrived at our meeting spot—the Coffee Bean at the food court of the Venetian, where the neon signs of the pizzeria and burger spot stood out amid the vaulted ceilings and brown and tan terrazzo tiles—the situation felt surreal. As I sipped my tea, I glanced around at the tourists and vacationing families who would be sitting just inches away from me as I made plans to begin having sex for money.

I couldn't have been more surprised when a pretty young woman wearing sweatpants, no makeup, and her strawberry blond hair in a messy ponytail approached me. "Are you Suzy?" she asked.

"Yes. Bridget?" I asked, holding out my hand uncertainly.

"I just finished a workout," she said, motioning at her clothes and grabbing a coffee before sitting down across from me like it was the most natural thing in the world.

I immediately liked her and felt, based on her casual prettiness and easy confidence, like we could be fast friends. I could feel her sizing me up, and although she smiled kindly at me, I sensed a streetwise wariness below her pleasantness.

"I really want to try this," I said. "I really do."

"But why?"

"Well, I was a professional runner for many years," I said.

"It could be very damaging for my reputation if anyone found out I was sleeping with a man who wasn't my husband. So this seems like a great, discreet way to do just that."

Bridget shrugged, as if to say that my concerns were no big deal. Clearly she hadn't heard of me. But if she didn't entirely understand the reason behind my decision, she was definitely receptive, gazing at me warmly as she continued to evaluate me.

"This is going to be great," she said. "You're in your forties. I get so many clients calling, asking for an older woman. You could be in high demand if you want to be."

I liked the sound of that.

"I live in Wisconsin, so it'll only be something I do when I'm able to get away," I said. "And if possible, I only want to see your most discreet, high-end clients, so I can be sure no one will ever find out."

"Not a problem," she said. "It's all very discreet. We work with many celebrities and professional athletes. And we thoroughly screen all of our clients. One of our top clients happens to be in town this weekend. He's very handsome and very wealthy, and he's a cowboy. Literally."

"Wow," I said, already excited by the thought of who this man might be.

"He's going to love you," she said. "You're gorgeous, and you have a great body. And you're not just some young girl who can't hold up her end of the conversation. You're going to do well."

I'd always loved being coached, and I responded to the inspiring words and encouraging tone now. With each trip to

Vegas, my confidence had grown. Now I *really* felt good about myself. "Thank you," I said. "I can't wait to get started."

"I'll probably have an appointment for you soon," she said. "I'll try and arrange something for you while you're here. And if I know the dates when you'll be back, then I can just schedule you. When a client is calling in to make an appointment, we'll check to see if you're available. Get a disposable phone."

After my meeting with Bridget, I met Mark out by the pool at our hotel. He looked up when I sat down in the chaise next to him, but he didn't speak. I wasn't sure how much I should tell him, but I was too excited to stay silent.

"I'm really happy with how it went," I said. "I was well received. Bridget liked me, and she thought this could work."

The expression on Mark's face didn't exactly look like he was thrilled for me.

"I'm glad you're happy," he said neutrally.

THE NEXT DAY, A FEW hours before I was due to run the Rock 'n' Roll Marathon's first ever Stiletto Dash, which was to be held on the casino floor at the Palazzo, my throwaway phone began to buzz. I felt a corresponding vibration inside of me.

"Can you make an appointment in an hour?"

The Stiletto Dash was two hours after the appointment, so as far as I was concerned, that would work perfectly.

"Absolutely," I said, vibrating at a higher and higher frequency. "Can you tell me anything about the client?"

"This is one of our best clients," she said. "The cowboy I

mentioned to you. I think it would be good for you to start off with him."

Oh my gosh, one of her best clients. She's already giving me her top clients.

"Great," I said.

She gave me the details of where and when, how I should be dressed, and what I should expect from our time together. That was it. I was in.

The next thing I knew, I found myself in our hotel room at the Venetian, scrambling to get ready for my first appointment as an escort, while Mark lay stretched out on the bed, checking his e-mail. I looked at my phone and realized I had to be at Caesars Palace in just a few minutes, and I had no idea where it was.

"Mark, you have to take me to Caesars," I said. "I don't know where it is."

He looked up at me for a long moment, sighed, and then sat up and explained to me where I needed to go. I thanked him, gave him a quick kiss good-bye, and that was it. I left my husband of more than twenty years in our hotel room and went to have sex with a stranger for money. I hurried down in the elevator and stepped outside to find that the taxi line was impossibly long. Sprinting down the Strip, I dodged baby strollers, bachelorette parties in short shorts, and heavy-set tourists with their cameras out. And then, suddenly, there I was at Caesars, with its extravagant pool with the tropical blue bottom and the Greek statues and leaping fountains. I stopped. And then, totally relaxed, I turned and walked toward the casino entrance.

Bridget had explained that my first client was a forty-seven-year-old cowboy named Paul who was in Vegas for the weekend rodeo, that he was incredibly wealthy and one of the service's top clients. That's all I knew about the man I was about to have sex with. And yet, by the time I found myself standing in the hushed, womblike hotel corridor, all I felt was comfortable and excited. I was dressed in the tight little black dress the chef had bought for me, which I'd worn with the only high heels I had, a pair of conservative black pumps from my motivational speaking gigs. I hadn't yet learned how important it was to dress the part, that as an escort my clothes had to create a certain air of wealthy glamour that was an essential part of the fantasy for our clients.

I was thrilled when a very tall, handsome gentleman with salt-and-pepper hair responded to my knock, opening the gigantic double doors onto the biggest suite I'd ever seen, with elaborate chandeliers and a tile floor that resembled marble. I stood on the threshold for a beat, posing for him.

"Oh, you're so beautiful," he said.

I knew my role in this play: to please this man and be his best companion ever. I followed him into his huge suite. I was determined not to let on that I'd never seen anything so fancy in my life. Instead, I focused on acting cool. At his suggestion, I sat down at a large glass table, unaware that he would soon be having me on its cool, smooth surface. He poured me some red wine.

As I took the glass from him, I slowly crossed my legs, feeling powerful now, as I absorbed the intensity with which his eyes followed my every move. He took the chair across from me, staring at me openly, as if he was trying to figure out who this woman sitting across from him was. Bridget had told him this was my first time, and that had been the draw for him, but again, I tried not to give up my power.

"So you're in town for the rodeo?" I said. "That must be exciting."

"I come every year," he said. "Good for business. Good for pleasure."

"Good for *me*," I flirted.

"How do you keep your body in such amazing shape?" he asked.

I was prepared to lie about myself, and the words flowed out of me easily.

"I was a college gymnast," I said.

"Is that so?" he asked, sounding excited. "I'll bet you were good."

The conversation happened so easily it was like he was an old friend. He was very confident and soon put me at ease. The sex started just as naturally. He was the aggressor, maybe because he was aware that I was new at all of this, and he quickly stripped me out of my dress. Before I knew it, I was naked, my back pressed against the cold glass of the table where we'd just been making small talk. I became so caught up in the sex and the power I felt from giving him pleasure that I forgot to watch the clock. The next thing I knew, more than an hour had passed. If he'd noticed we were running over, he'd kept quiet.

"Oh, I have to go, because I'm here doing work for the

marathon," I said, feeling like I was enhancing the mystery surrounding my identity, never thinking such a revelation was reckless, or realizing clients had a tendency to try to find out everything they could about the girls they liked. "I need to leave right now. I can't be late."

"Well, then, we don't want you to be late," he said.

After I quickly showered and dressed, he handed me a white envelope of money and stepped closer, towering over my petite five-foot-four frame. My heart was pounding, as if I'd just finished a race, heat coursing through every inch of my body.

"Can you stop by for a couple of hours tonight?" he asked.

"Of course," I said.

I beamed up at him. *You have to be kidding*, I thought. *This is so easy. And fun. And I will get paid a lot of money.*

He opened the door, and as I left, I paused to kiss him good-bye.

"Call the service about tonight, and I'll try to be back," I said.

As soon as the heavy double doors of his suite shut behind me, I hurried to the elevator, eager to open the envelope he'd given me and see exactly how much money was inside. One by one, I flipped through the hundred-dollar bills, growing giddy as I counted ten. My rate was five hundred dollars an hour. He'd literally paid me double! My high zoomed even higher. That was it. Another switch had been flipped.

Thinking about Mark waiting for me at the race dampened my euphoria. I didn't want to tell him any of the details of what had just happened, or how easy it felt to be Kelly. I *was* Kelly now, a whole different person. This was the name I had chosen for myself, but it was more than that. Kelly was my new personality—this confident, powerful woman who was in control and made her own decisions. There was no way I could ever go back to being the woman I'd been. And I didn't have to. I was in charge, and I would keep the details to myself.

Chapter 12

ATF

After the appointment, I literally ran down the strip in my bare feet with my heels dangling in one hand. Even though the strip was jammed with people, as usual, I didn't see anyone around me. I arrived at the Palazzo just in time, ready to win this silly race.

The casino was packed with women in their high heels, looking nervous about the possibility of falling on their faces as they waited for their turns to sprint seventy-five yards to win the five-thousand-dollar first prize. With so many women packed in amid the dinging bells and flashing lights of the casino floor, I had a hard time finding Mark standing by the starting line, as I had instructed him, holding my tight black shorts and tank top. I rushed up to him.

"They're looking for you at the start," Mark said.

"Okay, I'll get over there," I said, ducking into a nearby bathroom to change.

At the starting line, I looked down the row of girls running with me. We were all a special part of the event, the final race of the evening and the celebrity heat that wasn't allowed to be in on the prize purse. I recognized several girls from sexy B movies I'd seen. They were so stunning, in their short skirts and flowing, styled hair. Now I felt like I really had to stand out. Beneath my tank top, I had on the sexy bra I'd worn to my escorting appointment. I yanked my shirt off and tossed it on the ground. *I won't be needing that anymore.* Standing there in my black bra with silver metallic accents lining its rim, I felt completely comfortable and normal. In fact, I was having a blast. At this moment, my two worlds collided. I was at a race. I was running, but I was running in a bra and heels. It was perfect, the moment when the two sides of my life became one. I'd raced a million times with my parents, my coaches, Mark assessing my every move. I'd been made to feel ashamed for getting attention for my looks. I'd said no to *Playboy*. I'd had a breast reduction so I could look the part of the perfect athlete. I'd stopped selling my calendar when my father raged with embarrassment. I'd been humiliated in front of the entire world in the Olympics, not once but three times. I was done with all that. Now I was going to race my way, on my terms.

I won the race easily, and although I couldn't collect any prize money, I reveled at being in the center of the cheering throng. I barely registered Mark's presence, somewhere behind me in the crowd.

Just when I thought the day couldn't get any better, my disposable phone buzzed in my purse again. Bridget sounded excited.

"Paul called me after your appointment and said you're his ATF," she said.

"ATF?"

"All-time favorite," she explained.

"Oh, wow," I said. "Yeah, that was fun. He's really nice."

"Well, he must think you're really *nice*, too, because he wants you to come back tonight," she said. "I'm having dinner with Paul and his friend and they want you to join us."

"Really? That'll be great. Of course I'll be there."

I knew from our conversation the day before that Bridget had once been an escort herself, and I figured she was curious about this new woman one of her top clients had described as his all-time favorite. That was fine with me. I loved being praised, and it only increased my confidence. I couldn't wait. I was in overdrive. It was a relief that Mark was also off doing his own thing, watching the L.A. Kings downstairs in the Sports Book, so I didn't have to explain myself to him. It was already almost time for me to leave for my second appointment, so I didn't have as much time as I wanted to enjoy the process of getting ready, anticipating the pleasure of the encounter that was to come. I still really only had the one sexy outfit, which I had worn earlier in the day, and so I pulled on my most flattering jeans and a tight top, put on my makeup, and brushed out my hair until it was shiny and smooth.

I met Bridget, Paul, and his friend for dinner at the Palm, a restaurant at Caesars. She was dressed casually and clearly felt comfortable around the two men, who she had known for some time. I wasn't hungry in the least, but I loved the feeling of being wined and dined by the men in Vegas, so I was enjoying myself. We sat at a tall bar table and had dinner, laughing and talking like old friends. Toward the end of the meal, two young women in heavy makeup and short dresses approached.

"Hi, Paul," said the blond girl, her voice sexy and familiar.

"Hi, ladies," Paul said. "Nice to see you again."

"What are you guys up to tonight?" said the second woman.

I gathered that Paul and his friend had recently met these girls at the hotel, and now the women were desperate to hook up with them. I definitely sensed a gold-digging vibe. I certainly wasn't judging anyone, but I laughed a little inside. Clearly, these girls had no clue that there was no chance. Paul slid several crisp hundred-dollar bills into the leather sleeve containing the check for our meal.

"Sorry, ladies, we were just leaving," he said, standing up and waiting for Bridget and me to do the same before he turned to go, like a true gentleman. The girls exchanged a worried look, unhappy we were leaving without them.

As we walked out of the restaurant, they were close behind us, as if they intended to trail us into the elevator and back to Paul's room. *How do we get rid of these girls? We need to go. We're working.* An elegant solution popped into my mind.

"Will my husband please get over here?" I said to Paul.

He looked ready to laugh but strolled over to where I

was and put his arm around me. The girls then took off, just like that.

I was still learning how everything worked, and if I'd been a little surprised when Bridget had told me that she was friends with Paul, I was definitely surprised when she headed back to the room with us. But I was excited, too. Here was an all-new adventure for me to enjoy, whatever it might turn out to be.

This time, when Paul opened the door and welcomed us into his suite, I was ready for the grandeur and my nonchalance wasn't an act. I watched Bridget closely, wanting to learn how things were done by a true pro, noticing with interest the way she and Paul leaned in toward each other. He almost looked like her lover rather than a client, even though she didn't so much as kiss him on the cheek, and both he and I knew she had a boyfriend—a fact I'd been interested to learn after I'd begun working for the service—and wasn't going to be spending her night in that suite. I had thought I was going to be with Paul, so now I wasn't sure what was going to happen. But this didn't make me nervous. I liked the uncertainty.

I turned my attention to Paul's friend.

"Are you enjoying yourself?" I asked, echoing Bridget's casual intensity and walking right over and sitting down next to him, as if I'd known him for years.

"Yes, very much," he said, his voice low and husky with the stirrings of desire.

Bridget was flirting with Paul, even though she had no intention of sleeping with him, but I could tell she was keeping tabs on my conversation, and I gathered from the bemused look on her face that she was pleased. Paul handed me a glass of pinot, and from the first sip, I felt its velvety power snaking through my veins, already pulsing from the wine we'd had at dinner. After we finished our drinks, more drinks were poured, and it soon felt like a party. I was aware of Bridget observing me, and I definitely felt like I had to be at my best. Again, everything happened really quickly. I was the first one to get my clothes off, stripping down to my simple black Calvin Klein bra-and-panty set. I drank my wine and talked a mile a minute about how much fun I was having. I embraced the wild girl I'd long wanted to be. It felt so good. I went over to Bridget and we started kissing, which the guys definitely enjoyed, and then we just kind of paired off from there. Paul's friend grabbed my arm to lure me closer to him, and we started making out.

The next thing I knew, I was stripped completely naked, in bed with Paul's friend, who was also naked. This time, I was going to be the aggressor, and I made the first move, being sure to exude sexy confidence and high-energy fun. Not that I really had to do much acting. I was having the time of my life. Meanwhile, Bridget and the cowboy settled onto the other bed in the spacious room. When he finally realized they weren't going to have sex—not for a lack of trying on his part—they settled down and watched us, giggling the whole time.

I wasn't self-conscious in the least. If anything, being watched—and praised—turned me on even more. The fact that most people probably would have found the scene bizarre only added to my excitement. I wasn't most people anymore. I was Kelly. And the truth was, the capacity for this had been in me all along.

I had no idea what time it was or how long I was expected to stay, since we'd never talked about the specifics of this appointment. Finally, I realized it was getting late, and by the look of things, this could go on all night. I could feel the wine wearing off and it hit me that my husband was here in Vegas, too, and probably wondering where I was. I was lying naked in bed with Paul's friend, taking a break. I turned to Bridget.

"Do you mind?" I said. "I've got to go."

Bridget sat up in bed a little bit and turned to Paul. "Kelly's got to go," she said.

He nodded.

"I left an envelope for you in the bathroom," he said.

After retrieving my envelope of money, I said good-night to the two men. Then I walked into the lounge of the suite to get dressed, with Bridget following behind me. As she walked me to the door, she said, "You are something else. That was so much fun."

I was overjoyed—I had made two thousand dollars having a wonderful time.

"I'm here for one more day," I said. "And I'll be back soon."

"Great. I'll try to send something your way," she said.

I gave her a kiss and headed out into the hallway, wondering how Mark would be when I got back to our room. I found Mark sleeping, so I moved about the room as quietly as possible, taking a shower and then kissing him on his cheek and lying down in bed next to him, even though my body was still thrumming from the excitement of the day and sleep was the last thing I wanted.

The next day, Bridget again called me and told me that Paul wanted to see me one last time. I was thrilled that I'd made such a good impression on such a good client.

This time, when I walked along the hushed, elegant hallway to Paul's room, the path was familiar. I wasn't nervous at all when I stood waiting outside the enormous doors to Paul's suite, waiting for him to let me in. And then he opened the door, and as I seductively stretched my body up to kiss him, I could just see the room behind him. It was full of men. Not just his friend from the night before, but three other men. They were slightly younger and all wearing cowboy hats. As I stepped into the room it buzzed with the charged energy that happens when men and women are alone together and sex is on the horizon. The only question on my mind was how much sex, and with how many of these men.

If I had felt reluctant to share the details of my previous appointments with Mark, I *definitely* was not going to tell him about this one. I didn't feel that there was anything wrong with what I was doing. I'd enjoyed it, even. But I knew Mark would never let me come back if I told him. So I did my best to act normal when I rejoined him in our room and we packed up our luggage and prepared to leave.

We flew to Los Angeles, where Kylie was staying at Mark's parents' house in Malibu. After visiting for a few days, we traveled down to San Diego for an appearance I had agreed to make. The whole trip, I could not stop thinking about Vegas. Shortly thereafter, my disposable phone rang. It was Bridget letting me know that another top client wanted to meet me. I let her know I was on my way back.

AS I BEGAN DRESSING, TUCKED into my room back in Vegas, I immediately began turning myself into Kelly.

Although Kelly was definitely a real part of me that felt like it had always been lurking inside, wanting to get out, I also gave some serious thought to who Kelly was and how she should behave. And I soon made a surprising discovery. *She's just like Mary,* I thought, consciously modeling my new alter ego on my beloved best friend. Not that I could have ever pictured Mary as an escort. But I'd so admired Mary for being such a strong, independent, witty badass who always spoke her mind and didn't care if people agreed with her or not. Most important, Mary had used her voice, quitting running when it no longer inspired her and fighting her cancer on her own terms, even in her final days. I wanted to be like that, too—or I wanted Kelly to be like that.

My client this time was staying at the Mandalay Bay. I happily walked through the frantic casino floor on my way to the elevator bank, thrilling when I felt men's admiring glances trace the lines of my body.

When I got upstairs to the client's suite, I was met by a good-looking, very wealthy corn farmer from the Midwest, Bob, who was in his mid-sixties. He had sexy silver-gray hair and a confident, seductive air about him. As had become the norm, I approached him as if he was an old lover who had been looking forward to a reunion. He seemed pleased. He had paid for two hours, and instead of getting naked right away, he wanted to go down and gamble. I knew my role and walked proudly by his side, giving him the thrill he wanted, being able to walk through the casino with an attractive, much younger woman by his side. He sat down at the hundred-dollar slots, pulling out a roll of hundred-dollar bills and eagerly sliding the first one into the slot. I perched on the stool next to him, carefully adopting my most seductive pose.

"Good luck," I said as he pushed the button to operate the slot.

But he didn't win, and before I knew it, he'd lost two thousand dollars. Shrugging like he was bored, he stood up. *You lost two thousand dollars like it was nothing. Could you just give that to me instead?* I thought, but I didn't say a word.

"Come on, let's go get a drink," he said.

I trailed him into the bar, where he ordered me a glass of pinot and we sat down at a small table together.

"So what brings you to Vegas?" I asked.

"Business," he said. "I'm in the corn business, and I'm here with my friend who produces the seed I use to grow my corn."

"Fun," I said. "Do you guys travel a lot?"

"Yeah, we both need to get away from home. I'm married," he said, as if the marriage explained why he needed to get away as much as he did.

"You're not happy?" I said, feeling like I could really connect with him.

"Not anymore," he said. "Not for a long time. My grandkids make me happy. They're great. But my wife? Don't ask. Sometimes I travel with a woman I know from Denver. Maybe you and I could take a trip together sometime."

"I'd like that," I said.

"Have you ever been to Denver?" he asked.

"Oh, sure, a bunch of times," I said. "I've been all over the West and the Midwest. I went to the University of Wisconsin."

"Really?" he said, his voice sounding excited.

I was too new at escorting to know that the men coveted information about the girls they saw because it made them feel like they had special, favored status. And I hadn't yet learned to be careful about my words. I didn't want to be just another random escort. I wanted to forge a connection with my clients, to make it feel like we were friends; that connection was a huge part of the turn-on for me, and without it I felt less of the thrill of the moment. After we finished our drinks, we went upstairs to his room. I was quickly naked and on my hands and knees on the enormous bed. Somewhere along the line, without thinking about it, I referred to myself in the third person.

"Come on, Suzy . . ." I said, and then my voice trailed off as I realized what I'd done. But I quickly carried on as if nothing had happened, hoping he did not catch it.

I noticed that he was watching me very closely, but I figured there was no way this man could piece together who I was with so little information. There were a lot of Suzy's in the world. How would he know which one I was?

I wanted to win at my new game, which in this world meant having many repeat clients. My strategy was paying off. Bob seemed to have an amazing time, and before I could leave, he was already making plans.

"I want to see you again," he said.

"Yes, of course," I said.

"I want you to be my regular girl," he said. "I'm not going to see any other escorts."

"I like the sound of that," I said. "Next time, go ahead and text me and we'll set it all up."

This was exactly what I was looking for: to be the best, and I was thrilled.

◆ ◆ ◆

Being bipolar means being insatiable. The high of the mania is never high enough. There is always a desire—a need—to push the high to the next level, in the same way that a drug addict constantly requires more and stronger drugs. For a person with bipolar disorder, risky behavior can be the best drug of all. And there are particular kinds of dangerous activities that feel better than others; sexually provocative behavior is near the top of the list. Also up there are spending large sums of money, and taking drugs and drinking alcohol. In a way that someone without bipolar disorder may have difficulty understanding, there is no longer any voice of reason that can assess the potential negative consequences or stop the behavior. Much like a teenager without any impulse control, a person with bipolar disorder can only see the immediate positive outcome of feeding the high: it will feel good. Everything else—family, friends, employers, safety—falls by the wayside in pursuit of the high. My own time in Vegas is almost like a textbook case of untreated bipolar disease, and for those who wonder how a small-town midwestern girl married to her college sweetheart could have gotten so far out of control, there's your answer right there. Along with my other symptoms of bipolar disorder came a drive to engage in risky behaviors that never would have occurred to me before, from jumping out of an airplane and working as an escort to daytime drinking and spending thousands and thousands of dollars on clothes and jewelry and miscellaneous crap I didn't really need. While I was in Vegas, my bipolar disorder drove me on endlessly.

Chapter 13

BECOMING KELLY

W e spent the holidays in Malibu with Mark's family, as was our tradition. And then I faced the harsh reality of another miserable January in Wisconsin, another round of showings, new listings, and arguments with Mark because I couldn't focus on my real life. The very prospect was unbearable to me.

When I had to hold an open house for one of our properties, I'd grit my teeth and fake a smile for prospective buyers while thinking to myself: *If I were in Vegas, I would have made five hundred dollars for this hour of work, and I'd actually enjoy the hell out of it.* This seemed like a waste of time.

When Mark and I were alone, I didn't talk about Vegas

202 ◆ Fast Girl

much. When I did, it was with the goal of alleviating his concerns by reassuring him that I had everything under control and was nothing but happy with my newfound independence.

It's odd, looking back now, that my husband didn't put his foot down to make me stop. I'm aware that he now regrets consenting to my requests, but I think he knew that nothing could have stopped me at this point. More than that, he wanted more than anything to keep the peace in our household. He saw that I was happier than I'd been in a very long time. He was glad to see that I still had the capacity for happiness, as it had been a rare commodity in our house for a long time. He wouldn't have chosen being an escort as the source of my joy, to be sure, but slogging through the mundane routine of another Wisconsin winter was clearly not going to replace it, that was certain. One of my only distractions that winter was texting Bridget, which I did from time to time. I was grateful for this connection to the life that felt more real to me now, even when it was so far away. When I asked Bridget for advice about what steps to take next in my life as an escort, she suggested that I create my own page on the service's website, with which I could attract prospective clients. Then, she suggested, I could fly into Vegas specifically to do a photo shoot for the site. I liked the sound of that very much, and pushed Mark to let me go.

"Absolutely not," Mark said.

"No one will know it's me."

"Except for the fact that your picture will be all over it."

"There's a way they can do the pictures so no one will know it's me," I said. "They can blur out my face."

"I think it's a really bad idea, Suzy," he said.

I let the subject drop. These kinds of exchanges were normal for us these days. We were constantly bickering about some detail related to our business, our daughter, or our home. We did our best to stay out of each other's way. All of it just made Vegas that much more alluring.

And then, one day in early January, I got a text from Bridget, inviting me to take part in a meet and greet they were hosting for their best clients. As she described it, the girls dressed sexily, but not scandalously so, and spent the evening chatting with clients, giving the men a chance to meet them all and see which ones they liked. I *really* wanted to go to this. The image in my mind fit right into the fantasy I was constructing: a classy, dimly lit affair with soft music in the background, everyone flirting and drinking good wine. And that's how I described it to Mark. He had taken to repeatedly reminding me of the extreme risk that I might get caught, and just how devastating it would be for our daughter and our business if I did. But I was sure there was no chance of this. Vegas was the one thing in my life that I truly felt like I could control. I think after the debate over posting my photos on the service's website, Mark felt tired of fighting. But, once again, he objected on the grounds that the meet and greet was dangerous from a discretion standpoint. In truth, I think part of the draw for me was that it did feel a bit risky, and I liked that, but I certainly wasn't going to admit that to my husband.

"I'll make myself look completely different," I said. "Nobody will recognize me."

"It's your funeral," he said.

Nevertheless, I was overjoyed to be going. This would be the perfect chance for me to stand out. I went online and bought a tight, short, silver and gold dress with a very low-cut back. I booked two nights at Mandalay Bay and prepared for whatever would happen next. Once I arrived, I set about getting ready for the meet and greet. I loved the way my new dress clung to my skin, and the thought that a new client might be stripping it off me in just a few hours. Bridget had told me there was a really good chance I'd be working that night. All the better. That's what I was there for.

I climbed into a taxi outside my hotel and gave the driver the address Bridget had provided. I was surprised as we drove farther and farther away from the Strip. It was hard to picture the kind of cool nightclub I'd imagined, with the sexy lighting and the soft music. A few minutes into our drive, the driver got lost. He had no idea where we were, now that we weren't on the Strip anymore. I laughed and gave him the address again.

Finally, he found the place and pulled up out front. It was a large villa, its yard landscaped with pretty rocks in lieu of grass due to the desert climate. Casual as could be, I strolled up to the garage door, which was open, where a bouncer greeted me. I was there early to make use of the hairdresser and makeup artist the service had provided. I wanted to look my best for the VIP clients. I wanted to be the one they chose out of all the other girls who'd be there. The caterers were still setting up, laying out food, drying glasses. I settled into one of the six bedrooms and had my hair and makeup done.

The whole time, girls kept coming up to me.

"Oh, I love your dress," said a petite brunette with very tan skin.

"Thank you," I said. "You look cute, too."

By this point, I was feeling confident and excited for the night to start. There were about a dozen other girls from the service there, and I was sizing up my competition when I saw a familiar face across the room. It was Pearl. When she looked my way, I smiled and nodded at her, not sure whether she recognized me or not. But I didn't have any urge to go over and talk to her. Now that I was an escort myself, I understood how she had carefully created the mood during our threesome, making it feel like she and I had a special connection. I now knew that she had made me feel special because that was her job, something I now tried to do with each of my clients.

I continued to survey the selection of extremely attractive, extremely sexy women who were now my peers. A few of the younger girls stood together talking in high, excited tones, but most everyone else was a bit on her own, wanting to be available for conversation and flirtation—and more—when the clients began arriving. Most of the girls were younger than me—in their twenties or early thirties—but there was one woman who was obviously my age, maybe even older, which comforted me. I wasn't there to talk to the other girls. Although the girls were sweet, and I did make friends with a few of them, that's not what I was there for. I was there to stand out as the most desirable among all of them.

I went to the bar for a glass of pinot noir. Sipping my wine, I paced through the six bedrooms. I couldn't get over how different this was from what I had imagined. It felt more like a cocktail party in the suburbs than an exclusive event for a service's most valued high-end clients.

And then the men started arriving, along with one couple. I thought that a bit odd. But then again, nothing really seemed odd in this new world.

I eventually grew tired of standing, so I boosted myself up on the counter of the bar area in the living room and very slowly and deliberately crossed my legs, showing a great deal of skin. *Now I'll definitely get noticed,* I thought. And I did. I could feel the men's eyes collectively swivel over to me and linger on my extremely toned legs. I felt power coursing through me, the lack of inhibition, the desire to stand out, be noticed and admired, and I tossed my hair back to complete the impression I was making.

A short, middle-aged man in a sports coat was standing a few feet from me. He quickly crossed the room to where I was sitting and introduced himself. I took the hand he extended and held it an extra beat.

"I'm Kelly," I said. "It's a pleasure to meet you."

But it wasn't really a pleasure to meet him, because he turned out to be very dull, going on at length about something to do with business that I didn't entirely understand. Another, cuter man approached and cut in.

"Hello," I said, turning away slightly from the first man, who gave me one last lingering look and turned to talk to a tall girl with amazing curves. So it went.

I had chatted with several men when a tall, very good-looking man with dark hair approached me. Behind him were two of his friends, who were with two of the other girls from the service.

"Hi, I'm Kelly," I said.

"Wayne," he said.

"And where are you from, Wayne?" I asked.

"I own a software company in Los Angeles," he said.

"I love L.A.," I said. "I spend as much time there as I can."

"Really?" he said. "Well, maybe you'll have another reason to go there now."

"I hope so."

As he leaned in closer, I could smell his aftershave and feel the heat coming off his body beneath his light dress shirt.

"Do you want to go?" he said. "We're going to have a party back at our hotel. My limo is outside."

Now *this* was what I had been waiting for: a smart, successful, handsome client who had specifically chosen me from among the ten to twelve girls at the party. My body buzzed with the now familiar high. We climbed into his limo, just the two of us, and were whisked back to the Strip.

His friends took their girls back to their rooms, and we went into his suite alone. He had the lights off, and the sparkling expanse of the Strip shone through the window, faintly lighting the room around us. He had a beautiful suite, and he made me feel welcome right away. As he poured me a glass of wine, we chatted, getting to know each other. I was finding that this was another important part of the interaction for me, because when I was able to make a mental connection, it heightened the sexual connection that much more.

"So what do you do for fun in L.A.?" I asked.

"Well, I have kids, so that's a handful."

"I can imagine," I said.

"I've been married twice," he said. "The second time to a stripper, actually."

"I'll bet that was a trip," I said, relaxing a little more.

By the time I had my wineglass in hand, my dress was off, and things escalated from there. I ended up staying for two and a half hours. When I was in the bathroom getting dressed, I caught sight of myself in the huge mirror, which stretched across one entire wall. I hadn't had much of an appetite since I'd started coming to Vegas regularly, and I'd lost weight. My new dress kissed my curves and glinted in the light. I snapped a selfie, careful to cut off my face, so I could send it to Bridget for the website. I didn't care what Mark thought. I already had regulars. With a page on the site I could attract more.

When I emerged from the bathroom, Wayne handed me a thousand dollars.

"You should get in touch when you're in L.A.," he said.

"Absolutely," I said.

"I'd like to maybe take you on a trip sometime, too," he continued. "I travel to Phoenix for work."

"Sounds fun," I said. "Stay in touch."

I kissed Wayne good-bye and bounced out into the night. As I headed back to my room, my phone buzzed. It was Bridget. "He really likes you," she wrote. "Nice work." The praise brought a rush of joy to my already spinning head. I loved my new life.

AFTER TWO NIGHTS IN VEGAS, and an appointment with another client on my second evening, I had to catch my flight back to Wisconsin. Going home was the last thing I wanted, but I wanted to show Mark the money I had made, so he could see how much I was worth in Vegas. He certainly didn't seem to think I was worth much when I was home. As soon as I climbed into the passenger seat when he picked me up at the airport, I pulled the bundle of hundred-dollar bills out of my purse and held them up for him. "Here's what I made," I said.

Mark barely looked at the money in my hand and didn't say a word.

"I saw this guy named Wayne from Los Angeles who owned a software company," I said. "I met him at the meet and greet, and we took his limo back to the hotel where he was staying. He had the most amazing suite. I stayed for two and a half hours, and he paid me a thousand dollars."

"Uh-huh," Mark said, maneuvering the car through traffic.

"The meet and greet was so fun," I said. "I wore that new dress and all the other girls kept coming up to me and telling me how beautiful it was. There were like ten of us there. It was a little odd. I thought it'd be a nightclub, like really dark and sexy. But it was at this villa in the suburbs. About forty of the service's best clients were invited. It was actually kind of boring, just everyone talking and having drinks. So I hopped up on this counter and crossed my legs. And then everyone noticed me. All these guys in the room started talking to me."

"Really?" Mark said, looking at me intently.

"What?" I said. "I told you, it was a meet and greet. That was the whole point—to meet people."

"I realize that," he said, his voice growing agitated. "But I thought you would go in disguise or something. What happened to a couple of discreet clients, the whole fantasy-fulfilled thing? Someone is going to figure out who you are. And you don't seem to have any idea how serious that could be."

"You worry too much," I said, closing my eyes and wishing myself back.

Mark did occasionally make a good point about why he was so concerned. We were in our bedroom one night after Kylie had gone to bed, and I had Vegas on the brain once again. "You know that client from the Midwest?" I asked.

I thought I noticed Mark visibly stiffen, as if steeling himself. Not that I took the hint.

"The corn guy?" he said.

"Yeah, him. I don't think I told you this, but the weirdest thing happened when we were together in his hotel room."

Again, Mark's frame grew rigid, but I kept talking.

"I referred to myself in the third person, which is weird because I *hate* talking about myself in the third person. Only, I forgot I was Kelly, so I said 'Suzy' instead."

"You did what?" Mark said. "What if he figures out who you are? If anyone found out . . ."

Gee, if he's going to react like this, maybe I shouldn't tell him anything at all.

"Don't worry so much," I said. "Nothing's going to happen. I mean I told him I went to the University of Wisconsin, but it's not like he knew I was a runner there."

"Suzy, you can't do that," Mark exploded. "You don't understand how guys are. If they like a woman, they want to find out everything about her."

I had worked very hard to win Bob over, and I really hoped he did like me. I was sure Mark was overreacting. He worried way too much. It was his favorite thing to do.

"Mark, it'll be fine," I said.

"No, it won't be fine," he said, picking up our iPad from where it rested on the bed between us and typing a few things onto the screen.

"Jesus, Suzy, all I did was search on Suzy and Wisconsin," he said, handing me the iPad so I could see what had come up.

There it was: my entire running history. I couldn't believe it, but I also couldn't find it in myself to be worried. Nothing would happen. I was sure of it. My husband didn't understand; there was a code between my clients and me. We shared something special that no one else had access to. And they would never betray me. In fact, if Bob knew who I was, maybe he'd like me more. Maybe he could be even more helpful in attaining my new goal—to be the top escort at the service, maybe even in Vegas.

AT THIS POINT, I WAS only getting away to Vegas about once a month, and so I spent the next few weeks replaying scenes from my recent trips and fantasizing about what might happen on my next trip.

I was proud of the money I could make in Vegas, and to me, it was like a better, easier alternative than selling real estate. I just wished Mark could see it that way, too. We barely had sex anymore, barely talked about anything beyond Kylie—except when I needed him to approve some new aspect of my Vegas life—and avoided each other as much as possible. We fought less that way. At the time, I put all the blame on Mark. He was constantly accusing me of being selfish, and while I had become quite self-centered, putting my own happiness before the well-being of our marriage, family, or business, I didn't see it that way. Instead I resented him. He didn't support me. He didn't understand what Vegas meant to me. He wanted me not to be myself, but instead to stay the woman he knew in Madison who wore sensible shoes and picked up her daughter at school. I know now that he was simply trying to accommodate the fact that the woman he loved was finally happy, but the thing making her happy was taking her farther and farther away from him.

Eventually, I set up my web page after I showed Mark the photo I had taken in the gold dress, and he realized there really was no way anyone was going to be able to recognize me. And so I excitedly sent messages back and forth with Bridget to hammer out the details: my age, thirty-nine (well, really I was forty-three, but that wasn't such a stretch); that I was a business owner who could only be in Vegas a few times a month, but was devoted to making my clients very happy when I was there; my preferred drink (pinot noir or a lemon drop martini); and my preferred designers, Louis Vuitton and Christian Louboutin (even though I owned neither at the time), should a client wish to give me a gift. I couldn't wait for my page to go live. It was going to change everything.

During this time, I was also fielding texts from regulars, including Bob, who liked it when we sent dirty messages to each other and wanted to know when I'd be back in Vegas. At first, I didn't know what to tell him, but I kept him interested with sexy texts and promises of how fun our reunion would be.

Finally, my page on the service's site went up, and just like that I had enough business to merit another trip. I spent Valentine's Day in Madison with Mark and Kylie, but Mark and I weren't feeling particularly romantic by then, so we put all our focus on our daughter. She and I had a tradition of buying candy and writing Valentine's Day cards to all of the kids in her class. I sat with her at the dining room table, completing this simple task with my daughter, the only thing still rooting me to home.

As soon as I landed in Vegas, I put the finishing touches on my look. I'd learned by now that all the escorts got spray tans, and I booked an appointment at their favorite place. I also got my hair and nails done at my hotel. I realized that looking good was its own full-time job, but I actually enjoyed the process. I got a little thrill from seeing other women in the waiting room of the spray-tan salon, women I could tell were also escorts. I was impressed by how sexy and confident they all looked, and pushed myself to mimic everything about them. Later that day, when I had a photo shoot to generate more images for my personal web page, I reveled in the attention from the photographer. I was reminded of the request to pose for *Playboy* that I had been forced to turn down right after college. Olympic athletes didn't do things like that. Now, I could do whatever I wanted, and I happily stripped off all my clothes and struck a pose in just my lingerie. I felt so free. There were two other girls in the room, getting ready for their shoots, but I wasn't bothered by their presence. Being watched just made me feel sexier.

Chapter 14

I KNOW WHO YOU ARE

I loved the fact that I already had regulars, and I was excited to see Bob. When I walked into his suite, I kissed him with the passion of a lovers' reunion and perched myself on the edge of his couch, wondering what he'd want from me that day and eager to give it to him.

He seemed excited to see me, which I liked. He poured our drinks and then sat down close to me on the couch. I was expecting him to compliment me, maybe even say something sexy he wanted to do with me. Instead, he dropped a bombshell.

"I know who you are," he said.

"What do you mean?" I said. "I'm Kelly."

"Sure, when you're here in Vegas, but I put two and two together, and I know that you're Suzy Favor Hamilton when you're home in Wisconsin."

Mark had warned me, and I hated that he was right, hated being reminded of the old life I'd just pried myself out of. But I wasn't worried. I knew I belonged in this world and nothing bad would happen to me while I was here. Bob watched me eagerly, as if he was enjoying this moment, as if knowing my secret meant that our relationship was somehow special, deeper than any others I had.

"Don't worry," he continued. "I'll never tell anybody."

"I know you won't," I said. "I trust you."

"Good," he said. "You should. Now let's go get you some new lingerie."

I liked the sound of that. Having men spend money was now a big part of the thrill for me. The high was already building as we entered the shops at Caesars and approached the Agent Provocateur display window, with its mannequins in naughty poses in gorgeous lace. The store looked expensive and exclusive, and I felt very special as I walked in next to Bob, standing by as he flipped through the racks of skimpy lingerie with confidence, picking out pieces he liked and giving them to a saleswoman.

"She'll be modeling them for me," he said to the woman, nodding my way.

The woman, who was very thin and pretty enough to have been a model herself, gave me a knowing look. Instead of being embarrassed, I felt excited by the fact that she knew why we were there. I strutted along behind her into the fitting room as Bob sat on a small sofa to wait for my version of a runway show. As soon as I had the first bra-and-panty set on, the woman came into my dressing room to check the fit. Seeing her come up behind me in the triptych of mirrors was enough to turn me on, even before she'd put her hands on me to adjust the straps. It wasn't that I wanted to have sex with this woman, but I liked the attention, liked having her focused so intently on my body. When she had gotten the fit just right, I pushed open the dressing room door and, without a moment's hesitation, strolled right out into the store where Bob was sitting, not caring that I might be visible to other shoppers. Bob beamed at me.

"Holy shit," he said.

Head held high, wide smile on my face, I paused just in front of him, close enough that he could have reached out and touched me.

"I'll take that as a compliment," I said.

"Turn around," he said.

I made a slow circle, allowing him to admire every inch of my bare skin, which I knew was toned and tanned and ready for a close-up.

I modeled several combinations for Bob. Finally, I put on one that was made entirely out of black netting, which I found pretty strange, but as soon as he saw me, his whole face lit up. "That's the one that I like," he said.

I stood beside him at the cash register while the saleswoman wrapped the lingerie in tissue paper and rang it up. The total for one bra and one pair of panties was three hundred dollars, more than I normally spent for an entire outfit. Of course,

Mark and I made good money selling real estate, and I'd done well as a professional runner, but it had never been a part of our lifestyle to pay that much money for decadent purchases like lingerie. This was a whole new thrill. I throbbed with the pleasure of the entire outing and the knowledge of what was to come when we got back to his hotel room and I modeled it for real.

From such a young age, I'd been told I was special, a prodigy, destined for greatness, and I had spent my whole life chasing that dream on the track. Now, in Vegas, I was looking to be number one, too. At first, it had been enough to have the men I slept with tell me how amazing I was. And then, when I'd needed to take it up a notch, having sex for money had been enough. Then my need to compete turned into wanting more and better gifts from my clients. Now, chasing the high, I became obsessed with the rankings that clients gave escorts on the go-to website for information about escorts all over the world, the Erotic Review. The rankings were the thrill for me, and they fed my insatiable desire to compete. Vegas was no different than the track. If I was going to compete, I had to win.

Formulating a plan of attack to climb through the rankings, I thought of regulars I could surely receive 10s from, and prepared myself to go the extra mile for new clients who, in turn, I trusted would write me a positive review. I wouldn't rest until I was number one in Vegas.

Meanwhile, I continued to text with Bridget, checking in with her about my schedule. Although I was never sure who was behind the service, she was the only person I ever dealt with there. And the longer I knew Bridget, the more

impressed I was by her and the more I liked her. She began
to show me the ropes, explaining that there was a schedule of
conventions to suggest which weekends would be the busiest,
so they could make sure the best girls were on hand to meet
the demand. In late February, she texted to let me know that
there was going to be a NASCAR race in Vegas the weekend
of March 10 and 11, and that I definitely wanted to be in town
because I could make as much as five thousand dollars for two
days. When Bob texted me to request an overnight when he
was in town for the race, that sealed the deal. I booked my
ticket. Mark didn't say a word.

AS THE PLANE DESCENDED, I could almost feel
the lights of Vegas waiting for me, reaching up into the sky
to welcome me home. To welcome Kelly home. She wanted
to come out in all of her sexy, fun, manipulative glory. She
couldn't wait to put on her black eyeliner and false eyelashes,
her Agent Provocateur bra-and-panty set, and her black high
heels. She couldn't wait to think only about sex. She couldn't
wait to be free. Finally, Kelly couldn't wait any longer, even
though we were still landing.

I pulled off the bulky sweater I'd been wearing to cover up
my figure in Wisconsin, revealing tight black leggings and a
tank top. I could hardly stay in my seat. It felt so small and
restrictive, and I felt so big and sparkly. *I'll show them how sexy
I am, and that I have all the power.* My heart beat even faster,
echoing off my breastbone. *Get me off this plane. I am so ready
to be the real me. I never was meant to be Suzy Favor Hamilton.
This is who I am.*

Toward the end of my time in Vegas, when my mania was at its most pronounced, I didn't want anything to pull me out of my high, and it became increasingly difficult for me to make myself go home to Wisconsin, or even think about the life I'd left behind there. But my normal life was going on while I was away. And now that I'm looking back on this period of my life from a healthy perspective, this is probably the most difficult part of my illness for me to come to terms with—how I temporarily abandoned my husband and daughter, and absented myself even further from my parents, making up lies when necessary to explain my absence.

Thankfully, I had a wonderful husband who was at home during this time, covering for me in every way possible. He made excuses for my time away to our real estate colleagues and family members, saying my public speaking career had taken off, removing me from home more than ever before. When I was gone, he got up every morning at six o'clock in the morning, began the day's work that would keep our real estate business booming, got Kylie up and off to school, devoted himself to all the demands of our business during a nonstop workday, picked Kylie up from school and took her to her various after-school activities, and made sure she was fed and bathed and fully loved before tucking her into bed again at the end of the day. Only to get up the next morning and do it all over again. When pressed by friends and family, he lied on my behalf, hid his unhappiness, and put on a brave face for the entire world to see.

I know this time was anything but easy for him, and it makes me so sad to think of him there all alone. I also feel terrible about lying to my parents, although I can see this was just my way of internalizing and continuing the cycle of denial and silence that plagued our family. This was how we'd dealt with Dan's illness when I was a kid. And this was how it happened all over again when I was an adult. Of course, none of us knew any of this back then. We were all just doing the best we could in the moment, no one more so than Mark, who earned my eternal gratitude by holding it all together during such a difficult time. I can only hope he becomes an example for other spouses and family members out there who are struggling to support a loved one who happens to be bipolar. You are not alone. It can and does get easier. And our family is very much rooting for yours.

Chapter 15
EXTREME

The next day, I spent the morning getting ready with extra care. My regular, Bob, was paying me thirty-five hundred dollars to do the overnight with him, and I had to make sure I had everything in order. When I was ready to go, I sat on the edge of the bed in my hotel room with my phone in my hand. I knew Mark expected me to check in, but I wasn't looking forward to the call. Finally, I took a deep breath and dialed.

I reassured him that I was safe and having a great time, and he caught me up on all the happenings of home. Mostly, we talked about Kylie, who was our only real connection at that point. After a few minutes, our strained conversation had run its course, and he put Kylie on the phone. In my brightest, most loving mommy voice, I asked her about school and gymnastics and told her I would be home soon. I could tell she didn't really understand where I was or why I wasn't with her, and her unhappiness momentarily shattered my illusion, leaving me feeling blue and guilty.

"Mommy has to go, Kylie," I said. "I'll talk to you soon and see you on Monday."

"I miss you, Mommy," she said, tears in her voice.

"I miss you, too," I said. "I love you."

The sound of her crying was too much for me. It reminded me how much I missed her and our old family life. For a moment, I lost my protective bubble of adrenaline and ecstasy. I didn't want that. I threw down the phone to finish getting ready. I wanted to get to the bar where I was meeting Bob as fast as I could. I needed a glass of wine and some of that Vegas glamour to feel like Kelly again.

It was a relief to spot Bob's silver hair as he snaked through the crowded bar at Mandalay Bay, clearly glad to see me, just as my first glass of wine hit my bloodstream. I liked that I knew how to please him—I had worn the set of black lingerie he'd bought me at Agent Provocateur—and I looked forward to doing just that once we got upstairs. And I liked that he was paying me thirty-five hundred dollars to spend one night with me. The bubble was back.

"Hi, beautiful," he said as he took the stool next to me.

"I've been waiting for you," I said, knowing he'd like the sound of that.

We watched the NASCAR race, which he and thousands

of racing enthusiasts had traveled to Vegas for, in a suite at the speedway where we had more drinks. By the time we went back to his hotel suite by helicopter, it was as if the call home had never happened. We spent an hour together in his suite, and he seemed pleased with every move I made. I was surprised when he started getting dressed. We had all the time in the world, and I assumed he would want to go again before we went down to the casino so he could play slots.

"I've got to go do some business," he said. "I'll be gone for three hours."

"I'll miss you," I said. "But I'll just go down to the bar and have a drink."

I hadn't been at the bar for more than a few minutes when I felt myself being noticed by five guys in the back corner. I smiled at them, and one of them took this as all the invitation he needed and came over to me.

"Hi, how are you doing?" he said.

"I'm great," I said.

After a few minutes of light conversation and flirtation, I'd been so friendly that he was smiling at me now.

"Come back and talk to my friend," he said.

When we reached the table, I could immediately tell which friend he meant, and I understood that he and another of the guys were interested in my services, while their other friends were very unsure. I quickly focused my energy on the two who were into it.

"You should come up to our hotel room," one said, a few minutes later.

"I'd love to do that," I said. "But I can only stay an hour."

"And how much would that be?"

"Three hundred dollars each."

By this point, I'd had enough conversations with the other girls to understand that there was no rule against lining up our own clients in our free time, and that it was actually very easy to meet a man in a bar in Vegas and get him to pay for sex. But because these men often hadn't planned in advance for the experience, they usually weren't willing, or able, to pay our normal rates. That didn't matter to me at all, nor did the fact that anyone I met on my own would not have been vetted by the service to ensure that he was likely to be safe, well behaved, and not a cop.

Within ten minutes of having met them, I was upstairs in their room, making sure both men felt included in the fun. We had just barely started to run longer than the agreed-upon hour when my disposable phone began to buzz. The message from Bob read: "Where are you, my dear?" *Oh, shit.* Here I was, naked in a hotel room with two other men. "I'm in the casino," I quickly wrote. "I'll be right there."

I threw my phone back into my purse, scrambled to find my clothes, which were scattered around the room, and pulled them on as quickly as I could.

"What are you doing?" they called out, not ready for the fun to end.

"You don't understand," I said. "I have a client. He's paid me for the full day."

"No, no, stay!" they exclaimed again and again, trying to convince me.

"You don't understand," I said again. "I have to go."

They finally gave in and paid me the money we had agreed upon, and I gave them my number.

I ran to the elevator and got myself back to Bob as quickly as I could, breathless and buzzed on the adventure and danger of it all, very pleased with myself. Now that I was Kelly, I made my own rules.

After dinner and a few more hours in bed, Bob was ready to go to sleep. He'd given me my own room in the suite for the night, which was nice. I was glad to have my own space because I was far too wired to even think about sleep. I was watching television when my phone buzzed.

"Come on, sneak out. Just sneak out. Another friend wants to meet you, too."

It was the guys from earlier. At that point, I would have much rather been out with them than with Bob, who'd gone to bed far too early for me and the fun, crazy night I'd wanted to have, but I knew better. I let them down gently and finally fell asleep. Living on the edge had finally worn me out.

I HAD ONE MORE APPOINTMENT on this trip, and it was one I was particularly excited for because it was my first threesome with a couple as an escort. The couple was celebrating their twelfth wedding anniversary. Given how life changing my own anniversary threesome had been, I wanted to make sure theirs was just as great.

When I got to Steve and Lois's room at the Palazzo, I was thrilled. They were a good-looking couple, and since I was now being totally open with myself about my attraction to women, I knew this would be fun. But when we sat down to have drinks and get to know each other a bit more, I could tell that this threesome had completely been his idea, and he'd had to talk her into it. Lois had only gone along with the idea because she loved her husband. I set about putting her at ease.

"So you're celebrating your twelfth wedding anniversary," I said, looking directly at her with as much warmth as I could. "That's quite an accomplishment."

"Yes, twelve years," she said. "He's the love of my life."

"You don't look old enough," I said.

"Well, we are," she said. "We have five kids."

"There's no way you've had five kids," I teased her. "What are you, an aerobics instructor?"

"No, I'm a teacher," she said, giggling. "We're both teachers."

I was glad to see her start to relax, and I took this as a cue to kiss her. When my lips first touched hers, I could feel her tense up, but then she gave in to the pleasure of the sensation and her body began to open on me. I did even more to put all the focus on her and allow her to ease into, and even embrace, this experience. Only, whereas my husband had held back during our threesome, sacrificing his own pleasure for mine, Steve did not take the same approach. He kept trying to insert himself between the two of us. It was nearly impossible to focus on her with him controlling everything, but I did my best. Even so, there was a moment during the session when she had had enough. She pulled away because he was paying more attention to me than to her on their anniversary. As soon as our time was up, I stood to gather my things. Steve abruptly went into the other room to get dressed, leaving her alone on the bed in a sea of rumpled sheets. She watched him leave and then hurried into the bathroom. I could see that she was crying. I'd wanted so much for her to enjoy the experience, and I felt terrible that I hadn't favored her as much as I should have, because I'd let him take charge. Her tears shook me—I didn't want to drive a dagger into their relationship, even if it hadn't really been my fault—and I vowed to never let this happen again. I had to be in control and focus on the woman, no matter what the husband did. I hurried in to her, her makeup smearing as her tears fell.

"Are you okay?" I asked. "What's wrong?"

"This is our twelfth wedding anniversary, and this isn't the way I planned our night to go," she choked out. "I never planned to have this threesome and be doing this on my anniversary."

I felt awful. This had clearly been his gift to himself, and in turn, it had ruined the night for her. I tried to cheer her up, but it didn't help matters when he came into the room, already dressed and whistling. He ignored her tears and continued to focus his attention on me.

"I'll walk you down," he said.

I looked over at her, feeling terrible, but my time was up, and I didn't see anything I could do about their marriage. I gave her a hug and dressed quickly.

"That was incredible," he said.

I looked at him out of the corner of my eye, wondering how he could be so indifferent to his wife's pain. It was clear he was having the same reaction I'd had to my first threesome. I was glad he'd at least enjoyed it, but I still felt terrible.

"It was, wasn't it?" I said.

When we were alone in the elevator, he leaned in close to me.

"Give me your number," he said. "I want to see you again as soon as possible."

I was guessing he meant without his wife, but I knew, as much as I wanted to help, it was really no business of mine. I gave him Kelly's number.

◆ ◆ ◆

When I was first diagnosed with bipolar disorder, I was given a list of common symptoms. It was like reading a description of my recent personality: hypersensitivity, talking a mile a minute, delusions, unpredictable mood swings, irritability, little need for sleep, racing thoughts, grandiosity, spending sprees. But none of the symptoms resonated for me more than this one: increased sex drive. And not only that, but a tendency toward risky sexual behavior with potentially dire consequences, along with all the other self-destructive activities engaged in by those with bipolar disorder. Up until that moment, it had been so hard for me to explain how I could have ended up working as a high-end escort in Las Vegas, not only to my family and friends and the public at large, but also to myself. No matter how depressed or stuck or unsatisfied I felt in my old life, how had I ended up acting out as dramatically and provocatively as I had? Suddenly, it was all clear. It wasn't Suzy who'd decided to become an escort in Vegas and thrived in this new hypersexual reality. It was bipolar disorder. It was the disease that brought me there and kept me there even when the risks to myself, and to my family, mounted and mounted. While I fully support my friends who still work as escorts and all the women who choose to be sex workers, and I have no shame about what I've done, understanding my own behavior has been crucial for me. It has not only allowed me to make sense of what I've done, but also, it's helped me to truly forgive myself for the pain I caused my family with my behavior. I have also come to realize that, while the life of an escort is not appropriate for me, I believe two consenting adults should be free to exchange sex for money, and so I cannot pretend to feel ashamed for having done something I don't think is wrong, just because it is taboo in our culture. That is my greatest hope for this book, to put an end to shame. And especially that anyone who suffers from bipolar disorder—or has a loved one who does—can finally set down the burden of shame related to any of the behaviors caused by the illness, or the illness itself, and finally focus on getting healthy and celebrating the many different ways there are to share our gifts with the world.

Chapter 16

MARRIAGE OF CONVENIENCE

W hen we got back to Madison, we returned to our new habit of staying out of each other's way. We were basically living in a marriage of convenience. Mark had come to realize that saying anything to me about my trips to Vegas or my behavior at home meant chaos, and chaos was something he did not want. He was considering everything from leaving me to telling someone about my double life, but he could not bring himself to do either. Trapped, he chose to cover, enable, protect Kylie and the business, and hope for the best, praying I'd eventually snap out of it and realize the recklessness of my activities. I stayed with Mark because he was my husband, and it seemed like maybe I really could have everything. We were married for the sake of being married, for the sake of our daughter, our parents, the business, and because we didn't believe in divorce, except as a very last resort. And so we both resigned ourselves to the reality as it was and realized we could actually live this way.

In a weird way, we were both getting everything we needed to get by. I was happier than I'd maybe ever been. And at that moment, Mark just wanted to work. Plus, he had Kylie. His family. In many ways, I realized, we were like the clients I was seeing. They wanted to stay married, so they stepped out in secret with an escort in order to avoid jeopardizing their marriage. We wanted to stay married, so we made an unspoken agreement to just do our thing.

By this time, I had enough regulars to justify a longer stay in Vegas. Even though spring was finally starting to show itself in Madison, my weeks there in snowy, frigid March had felt endless. And I was instantly ecstatic as soon as I landed in Vegas for my April visit, one of the monthly trips I was making to Vegas by this point. I'd texted my dates to Roger, a high-ranking military officer who was a favorite client now. He was my first for the weekend. He'd made a point to see me twice each of the two weekends I'd been with him before, in February and March, so by our fifth appointment, he really was beginning to seem like an old friend. Only this time, he surprised me, showing me that the life of an escort never exactly becomes routine. I strolled into his suite, kissed him hello, stripped down, and sat on the edge of his bed, always captivated by the view of the Strip, no matter how many times

I saw it. Instead of coming over to me, he went to the closet and paused for a moment. I looked at him curiously. The next thing I knew, he pulled out a long light gray fur coat.

"Why don't you go try it on?" he said.

"Thank you," I said, rubbing the coat against my bare skin.

I knew exactly what he had in mind, and I removed my bra and panties before sliding on the coat and letting it hang seductively open. I couldn't help but think of his mother, with her glamorous dresses and fur coats, who he'd told me about during all of our visits. It had become pretty obvious that the escorts he saw were filling some void for him, a void left behind when his mother died. I tried not to think much beyond that—if he was attracted to his mother I didn't need to know about it. I could tell he was in a lot of pain over her absence, and if this could make him feel better, I was happy to help.

When I modeled the coat for him, he was visibly excited, and he had me wear the coat for the rest of our time together. When I was getting ready to leave, he tried to pull me onto his lap to watch porn. I knew better.

"I'd love to stay, but I have another appointment," I lied.

"But I don't want you to go," he said, sounding like a cranky child.

"I don't want to go, either," I said. "But I have to. You know I can't be late."

"Can I see you tomorrow?" he asked.

"Of course," I said. "Just text me."

I was back in the clothes I'd worn to the appointment, and I turned to go, leaving the coat on the foot of the bed.

"The coat's for you," he said.

"Oh, wow, thank you," I said.

I pulled the coat back on with a dramatic flair, like it was the best gift I'd ever received, and gave him one last kiss before closing the door behind me. Once outside in the hallway, waiting for an elevator, I slid the coat off. I'd never been a big fan of fur, and it was already too hot in Vegas to wear it out on the Strip. But the extravagant gift was all that mattered.

I'd realized that most of the guys didn't need the incentive of an extra-long session to inspire them to write positive reviews. All I had to do was ask. I soon had my twenty reviews I'd needed to get ranked, and I was number two in Las Vegas. This was a huge thrill, and a sign for me that I'd made the right career choice. As far as I was concerned, this was as good as it could get. I knew number one, a voluptuous blonde in her thirties I'd been hired to do a threesome with. Her claim to fame was that she could come five times (or fake it five times, not that the guys knew the difference). She was gorgeous, incredibly sweet, and a total pro. I understood why all her clients loved her, and I knew I would never exceed her. This wasn't exactly easy for me to reconcile with my extremely competitive nature, but it helped some when I read my own client reviews like this one: "She is worth every penny. I will go bankrupt before I stop seeing her. I hope no one else goes to see her, because I want her all to myself. I never thought I would find anyone in this hobby like her." Then I learned that being number two in Vegas meant being number nine in the world. I hadn't even known they had world rankings. How was that even possible? Perhaps the biggest perk, though, was when Bridget informed me by text that my rate had just gone up to six hundred dollars an hour, of which the service would continue to get twenty percent, a fee I delivered to them every time I visited Vegas.

My trip to Vegas in June that year was just like the rest, and like all the previous trips, I loved every minute of it. From the time spent spray-tanning and getting my nails done, the conversations with bartenders I knew at the bars I frequented, and lunches with the girls who had become friends, I was in my element. I had worked and socialized enough with my fellow escorts to know that some, not the majority of them, could be extremely jealous and catty. But some impressed me with their success and power, much in the same way my clients did. I became friends with one woman who was a successful lawyer but enjoyed escorting so much that she flew into Vegas once a month to see a few exclusive clients. It was so fun to talk shop with these women, as they got the ups and downs of the job better than anyone else. One day in June I sat at the bar at Mandalay Bay, having lunch with my friend Lilly. We'd done a couple threesomes and had become pals.

"Do you live in Vegas?" I asked.

"Yeah, I do," she said. "You?"

"No, I live with my husband in the Midwest," I said. "I fly in a few times a month to see my regulars."

"Oh yeah, like who?" she asked.

I tried to think of my regulars who I knew saw other girls, too.

"Roger," I said. "He's in the military. I see him every time."

"Oh, yeah, I've seen him," she said. "Did he give you a fur coat?"

"Yeah, he did," I said, laughing.

"Me, too," she said, laughing as well.

From the beginning, escorting had seemed so normal to me, and it was a relief to talk to someone else who thought the lifestyle was normal, too. We ran through our lists of regulars without coming up with any other matches. And then, for some reason, I mentioned an Asian American guy I'd seen once.

"You saw him?" she exclaimed. "I saw him, too! He was so small, tiny."

We both cracked up laughing. I felt horrible, but I couldn't help myself.

"I know, I felt so sorry for him," I said. "He was so nice. I tried to make sure he had a really nice time even though . . ."

"I know, I felt bad for him, too," she said.

Not that nothing out of the ordinary happened. It's just that even the most outrageous behavior was becoming even more the norm for me. Threesomes were common, whether I was hired by a couple or hired with another girl from the same service. Sometimes I was hired with more than one other girl, like the time three of us were called in for a pool party at the adult pool at Mandalay Bay by a businessman who wanted to impress his clients, or the time four of us were brought in for four businessmen who had the suite at the MGM with its own private pool. There was the strip club addict, who took me out with him to watch girls dance and then got a lap dance right in front of me. The veteran who'd been shot in the stomach during the Iraq War and was overjoyed by our session because he hadn't known if he would be able to have an orgasm. The short Spaniard in town for the Electric Daisy Festival, a rave held at the Motor Speedway, who tripped on ecstasy during our session. The young professional golfer whose girlfriend liked to have threesomes but didn't know he was having an appointment with me. The even younger poker pro who'd just won his first big Vegas tournament and hired me to teach him about sex because he was being approached by lots of women now that he was rich and he didn't know what to do.

Even when things got dicey, I wasn't fazed in the least. I was usually very careful not to leave any of my belongings unattended or behind, especially not anything that could reveal my true identity. These were among the tips I'd learned from the other girls. I didn't bring my driver's license with me to appointments because men had been known to go through escorts' purses when they were in the bathroom. I paid attention to any computers visible in the room and casually threw a piece of clothing over them, just to make sure the guy wasn't secretly filming. I was a pro now—I had the whole thing down. I couldn't believe it when I accidentally left my iPad in the room of a client who I had picked up at a bar. Luckily, I was staying at the same hotel as him, and so when I got back to my room and realized what I'd done, I was able to quickly run over and knock on his door. He only had it in his possession for maybe three minutes, at the most. And when he gave it back to me, he acted casual, as if he hadn't even noticed it was in his room. But sure enough, the next day, he sent a note to my personal e-mail address. This was the third man to have found out who I was. The previous month, a regular who'd also gone to the University of Wisconsin had recognized me. And still, I wasn't concerned.

Chapter 17
NUMB

The action in Vegas slowed down considerably during the summer. It was too hot to attract the same crowds of tourists that flocked there during the winter. And there weren't as many conventions, which meant fewer doctors and businessmen looking to enjoy a weekend away from the real world. Also, Kylie was out of school and even busier with her many activities, including gymnastics, water ballet, and soccer. I stayed closer to home and helped Mark.

Being at home meant spending more time in close quarters with my husband, but we were far from close. I longed for my life in Vegas and tried to keep it with me by playing the same songs I listened to with my clients—like "Locked Out of Heaven" by Bruno Mars and "Numb" by Usher—over and over and over again until Mark couldn't take it anymore. I remained in constant contact with Bridget, several of the girls who were now good friends, and my most devoted regulars. By this point, I had plenty of clients who believed that I was their special girl, that I liked them more than any of my other clients and would eventually run away with them. I was able to leverage their affection into the promise of sessions with me if I booked a trip to Vegas. Sometimes when they texted that they wanted to see me and were coming into town, I would go so far as to tell them I'd fly to Vegas to meet them if they booked four hours with me. At least one person always agreed. The promise of even one appointment was enough for me to justify another trip back in July, and then if I got more business, even better. I always did get more business in the end, so it seemed like a good plan, an investment almost.

Along with my regulars—Roger and Bob—I had an appointment with a new client during that trip. All I knew when I met Lionel at the Double Helix bar at the Palazzo was that he was a lawyer from Kansas. From the minute I sat down next to him, it was clear he was smitten with me.

If he had felt connected to me in the bar, the feeling was amplified considerably in the bedroom. He was into blindfolds, ropes, and S&M, and I was open to all of it. Toward the end of our time together, he was lying on the bed staring at me.

"You don't know how incredible that was," he said. "I have sex with my wife maybe three times a year. She's having an affair. There's nothing I like about her anymore."

"I'm so sorry to hear that," I said. "That's terrible."

"I've seen plenty of gals in Vegas," he said. "But I'm only going to see you now, okay?"

"I'd like that," I said.

"Are you free tomorrow?" he asked. "I'd like to take you shopping. Who are your favorite designers?"

I paused for a beat, never wanting to seem too greedy, but wanting to seize the opportunity, too.

"Hervé Léger," I said. "Christian Louboutin."

"You'll look gorgeous in those," he said. "I want to buy you an outfit."

I floated out of there, high from the sex and already imagining the shopping spree.

That evening, when I got to Lionel's suite, he was jittery with excitement.

"I know who you are," he said. "You're Suzy Favor Hamilton. I remember seeing you run on TV, and I recently watched a show about you on the Big 10 network, and how you were one of the top twenty athletes in conference history."

"Lionel, you have to promise me you're not going to tell anyone."

"Of course I'm not going to say anything," he said. "I love you."

I nearly took a step back from him, I was so surprised. Even my most devoted regulars never used the word *love*. And this was only our second session.

"That's so sweet," I said, trying to keep it light.

"I'm serious," he said. "I want you to visit me in Kansas. I want us to know each other in our real lives. In fact, you should marry me."

"Lionel, if you know who I am, than you must know I'm married," I said.

"Well, not happily, if you're here now," he said. "Leave him and marry me. I'm serious. I'm a lawyer. I can give you everything you ever wanted. I'll totally spoil you. We'll go on vacation to tropical islands. We'll have sex twice a day, every day."

That was my cue to distract him by having a little sex right then. From that moment on, he was my most regular client, and my most devoted.

Mark and I were actually getting along better than we had in a long time. Our policy of giving each other space had led to considerably less tension around the house. And with me home more that summer, and with us bonded together in the complicated scheduling that went into getting Kylie to and from all of her events, we actually started getting along better than we had in months, maybe even years.

We celebrated my forty-fourth birthday as a family on August 8, picking Kylie up from her swimming lesson and then taking her to a day camp in our neighborhood. Kylie seemed excited to have us together and insisted on taking a picture of Mark and me before we left her with a sitter and went to eat at a fancy restaurant in downtown Madison. It showed us looking more relaxed together than usual, with me looking very skinny and very blond. Mark and I even had sex that night when we got home from dinner, and although it wasn't as passionate and loving as it had been years before, at least we were getting along.

The thaw between Mark and me meant that we actually started talking about subjects beyond simple household happenings again. And there was a great deal to discuss. One thing that had been weighing on Mark's mind was taxes. He'd slipped the small amount of money I'd earned from escorting in 2011 into our taxes for that year, but he knew he'd have to find a way to declare my much more substantial escort earnings for 2012, and he had no idea how to explain this to our tax accountant, or to the IRS.

Mark also dared to make a suggestion that he hadn't before. We were alone in our bedroom when he looked up from his iPad.

"Suzy, you need to stop," he said. "Too many people know who you are. It's only a matter of time until someone goes public. It's just too dangerous."

Mark had said this before, but he'd always stood by and let me continue.

"I can't stop," I said. "I've never been happier."

He looked at me sadly. Of course I'd been happier on my wedding day and the day Kylie was born, but those were both a long time ago, and this was different.

"You've got to see a psychologist," he said. "You have a history of depression."

I tell him I'm happy, and he tells me I need a doctor. Who does he think he is?

"I'm finally independent," I continued, trying to win him over to my point of view. "Nobody will ever know."

Finally, he gave up.

It was the last night I was home for a long time.

Chapter 18

MARRY ME

When I next saw Lionel, he had another gift for me. He gave it to me over dinner, sliding the flat box across the table as we sipped our wine. Many of my clients had very specific fantasies they wanted me to act out with them, and I was happy to explore whatever. But Lionel's desire wasn't sexual. He wanted me to be his wife, in real life, so when we were together, without ever explicitly saying that's how it would be, I pretended I was.

"You look so beautiful tonight," he said. "I have something for you."

I was already feeling the rush from the sleek lines and hushed glamour of the expensive restaurant and the intoxicating properties of the wine and his praise. My pulse quickened when I opened the box and rested my eyes on a beautiful diamond necklace. He'd already given me a sexy Hervé Léger dress and an iPad, even though I'd told him I already had one, but expensive jewelry was the most potent symbol of all I wanted my new life to be.

"Thank you," I said. "I love it."

"And I love you," he said.

And then he stepped out of the fantasy, as he sometimes did, forcing me to pay attention in order to keep up with what he wanted from me.

"I'll give you anything you want," he said. "Gifts. Vacations. I can provide for you in a way your husband can't. You wouldn't have to be here in Vegas anymore."

As if I'm in Vegas for the money, I thought.

I knew I wasn't going to leave Mark, wasn't going to marry Lionel, wasn't going to stop escorting, but I was flattered by Lionel's passion and persistence.

"That's very sweet of you," I said.

"We can be so happy together, Suzy," he continued.

I flinched a little at the sound of my real name. I didn't like hearing him say it.

"Help me put on my necklace," I said, eager for the mood to be flirty and light again. "When we get back to your suite I'll model it for you with nothing else on."

He came around the table, and I lifted my hair for him so he could slide the necklace onto my breastbone and clasp it behind my head. The gold was heavy and cold against my skin. I loved the weight of it and how substantial it felt: all those diamonds, all those dollars, the perfect emblem of everything he'd promised me.

It wasn't just my regulars who were upping the ante, either. I got a call from Bridget, preparing me for a date with a regular client.

"I've got this appointment for you," she said. "The date is with Jim. He buys expensive gifts for all the girls, so expect to go shopping. He's very wealthy."

"Excellent," I said, waiting for her to continue.

"Okay, have fun," she said, ready to get off the line.

"That's it?" I asked, wanting to know everything, like I always did, so I could add it to my notes. It was really important for me to know who I was seeing and how I could please him. Of course, Bridget didn't know about my notes.

"That's it," she said, again ready to hang up.

"But wait, what does he look like? What does he do? What are his special requests? What's he into?"

She sounded annoyed as she quickly ran through his basic information. I could practically hear her thinking, *What a pain in the ass. None of the other girls ask questions like this.* But I was number two in Vegas and the other girls weren't, so she humored me.

I was excited by the possibility of an expensive gift as I stood outside the door to Jim's suite. I prepared myself for some extreme sexual acrobatics. If he was going to buy me a gift, I was going to make sure he knew how much I appreciated it. When the door opened, a pleasant older man dressed in business casual met me with a wide smile.

"Hi there," I said, kissing him right on the mouth.

He stepped back a little and laughed.

"Oh, hi, Kelly, it's nice to meet you. Let's go get some dinner."

I was surprised that Jim didn't want to take a trip to the bedroom first, but I didn't let it show. I simply adjusted my behavior to match his calm, thoughtful mood. There was nothing the least bit sexual in our interaction as we made small talk on our way. He'd made a reservation at one of the top restaurants in Vegas, which impressed me, as did the fact that everyone from the hostess to the busboys knew who he was and greeted him with warm respect. I didn't know who this guy was beyond what little Bridget had told me, but I liked the feeling of being out with him. When it was time for us to be seated, he stepped aside a little and gestured that I should lead the way, like a true gentleman. Aside from letting it be known there were a few items I preferred, including pinot noir and lemon drop martinis, I always let the men pick our wine when we went to dinner, and often, our food. I was taken aback when he ordered a bottle of red wine for us that cost a thousand dollars. *My first thousand-dollar bottle of wine,* I thought, adding this to the list of incredible firsts I'd enjoyed lately.

"So do you come to Las Vegas often?" I asked him, wanting to know more about him.

"Some," he said. "I prefer to travel in Europe, but Vegas has its perks."

"I love Europe," I said. "Monte Carlo is my favorite."

"Yes, Monte Carlo is wonderful," he said, seeming a little surprised and very pleased that his new escort could speak knowledgeably of European cities.

Several times throughout dinner, I noticed him giving me a similar look over and over, as if he couldn't believe he was having such an intelligent conversation with me. Instead of feeling indignant at the implication that all other escorts were dumb, I thrived on the suggestion that I was unique and special. When the bill came, the meal itself cost a thousand dollars, plus the price of the wine. None of my clients had ever spent that much money on me for a meal, and I was flushed with pleasure and excitement. It was time to up the ante.

"Which store would you like to go to?" he said as we waited for the waiter to return with his credit card. "Chanel, Louis Vuitton, they're all here."

This is the best thing in the world, I thought. But I was not the type to be pushy when he was already being so generous.

"Which do you think?" I asked.

"How about Louis Vuitton?" he said.

"That's great," I said. "I don't have a really nice purse."

By the time we entered the Louis Vuitton store, with its elegant displays of expensive handbags, I could barely focus on even this extremely enjoyable task.

"Which one do you want?" he asked, smiling warmly at me.

Again, I hesitated, looking around. They were all beautiful. I didn't want to pick one that was too expensive when he had already been so generous.

"Which one do you think would be good for me?" I asked.

He surveyed the displays and picked out a beautiful handbag.

I beamed with joy, and I couldn't contain myself as we stood at the counter.

"This is my first expensive purse," I said to the saleswoman. "This is so nice of him. Oh my god!"

She laughed, not in a mean way, but as if she found it refreshing to see someone actually excited to be in possession of something so elite. I was so thrilled that I was lighting up that shop, and I could tell the woman loved me for it.

From there we went back to his room, and I stripped for him. We did finally have sex, but it only lasted for about fifteen minutes, and it seemed as if maybe it wasn't the point of the endeavor for him anyway. Jim wanted to treat a beautiful young woman to dinner at one of the city's most exclusive restaurants and feel her appreciation and admiration when he bought her an expensive gift she wouldn't have otherwise been able to afford. If that was what made him happy, I was more than glad to help give him what he craved.

By the time our appointment was over, I was vibrating with the combined effects of the meal, the conversation, the purse, and the feeling of having been acknowledged in some way by this very successful, very rich man.

"I definitely want to see you again," he said, cementing my happiness.

Later that month, I met with a client named Dylan, a wealthy techie who had sold his software company for major money and now enjoyed spending freely in Vegas on escorts and other pleasures. As we drank our wine before dinner, he began confiding in me.

"I don't feel like I have any choice but to come to Vegas," he said. "I'm in a sexless marriage."

"A lot of people are," I said, trying not to think about

Mark. "But it's good that you can take care of yourself. Does your wife know?"

"She didn't know for a long time," he said. "And then, recently, she found out and she actually gave me her permission. She just doesn't want to know when."

"That sounds like it's probably the best solution for both of you," I said.

I was at a nice restaurant, drinking an expensive bottle of wine, having a deep conversation with an extremely rich and successful man who I'd won over enough for him to tell me all about his troubled marriage. Not that long ago, each of these factors alone would have thrilled me, but now, they just felt normal to me.

"My limo's waiting outside to take us to my hotel," Dylan told me after we had finished eating and he had paid the bill.

I liked the sound of that. When we climbed into the hushed, opulent cocoon and pulled out into the constantly dragging traffic of the Strip, I kissed Dylan.

He paused and pulled back from me a little bit.

"There's something I want to give you," he said.

"What is it?" I said, already excited, hoping for jewelry.

He reached into his pocket and pulled out a small tube, from which he shook two white powder-filled capsules out onto his palm.

"One for you, one for me," he said.

"What is it?" I asked, a little wary.

"Ecstasy," he said. "It'll make you feel really good, I promise. I'll make sure you're safe. You just need to drink plenty of water."

That was enough for Kelly. She was up for excitement, risk, anything. Without further thought, I popped the pill onto my tongue and swallowed it. As the driver rolled the car past the great banks of sparkling lights that lined the Strip, we began to kiss, and I quickly stripped down to just my bra and panties. The partition between the driver's seat and the back of the limo began to go up, and I realized that the driver wanted to give us privacy. Suddenly, my high spiked that much higher at the thought of him watching us in the backseat.

"No, leave it down," I said, catching the driver's eye in his rearview mirror.

Dylan seemed as turned on by this as I was, because he pulled me onto his lap and took it from there. I'd found a way to up the ante once again.

MY CALLS HOME HAD BECOME ever more infrequent and brief. After his attempt to talk sense into me in the summer had failed, Mark seemed resigned to the fact that this was my life now. And if that was true, he had a new concern. During one of our rare phone conversations in September, he made me really talk to him.

"Suzy, you're in Vegas so much these days," he said.

I prickled, ready to get defensive at whatever came next.

"And the hotel bills are getting really expensive," he said. "It's ridiculous. Do you have any idea what you're spending?"

"But I need to stay at the nicest hotels," I said, looking around me at my room at the Encore. "A top escort out here has to present a certain image. And besides, I make a lot of money."

"That's all fine and good," he said. "But these bills are completely out of control."

I waited for him to tell me once again I had to stop, to come home, my defense at the ready.

"We should buy a condo in Vegas," I said.

Secretly, I was hoping this would be the first step in convincing him to move our entire life out west, but I knew I couldn't present it like that.

"It could be an investment property," I said.

"Right," he said, sarcastically.

Then, a few days later, he surprised me, obviously coming to the realization that this was going to be our life now.

"I've been thinking about it, and we should consider a condo at the Trump," he said.

"Are you kidding me? I love the Trump."

"The main thing is that you'll be safe, and we won't be spending so goddamn much money on hotel rooms," he said. "Hopefully, it'll be a good investment in the long run. I could let my real estate clients use it as a reward for working with us."

"When are you going to buy it?" I asked, already prickling with excitement. Although I was proud of how much money I made in Vegas, it was almost like play money, and I never thought specifically of using it to cover my Vegas expenses. I spent as much as I wanted in Vegas and what was left sat in our safe at home, untouched.

"I've already picked out the condo I think is best for us," he said. "I want you to go check it out, and if you think it looks good, I'm going to make an offer."

As I strolled through the condo, snapping pictures to send

to Mark, I felt a deep sense of satisfaction, like I was exactly where I was supposed to be. Maybe everything would really work out the way I wanted after all.

I DIDN'T HAVE TO DO everything a client wanted on a date, only what I was comfortable with, and the decision was totally up to me. At the same time, there were certain sex acts that cost extra, which the client knew up front. Mark and I had, in our old life, been very open when it came to sex. There was a lot I was comfortable with. And besides, there wasn't a judgmental bone in my body. I wanted to make my clients feel good and help them to live out their fantasies, and so I responded enthusiastically to almost everything they wanted to try. But there were a few things I wouldn't do, and that was that. No one ever tried to pressure me. But now that more and more extreme behaviors—drugs, taking high-end gifts, overnights—were becoming the norm for me, I had to push the boundaries even further. I started expanding the range of things I was willing to do, of my own accord. For a little while, at least, it worked.

When pushing the sex boundary lost its thrill, I started to occasionally tell clients who I was, so that by the end of my time in Vegas, probably a total of ten knew my real identity. When I did tell a client, I loved seeing how excited he got when he learned I was a famous runner who had competed in the Olympics. I didn't think about the risk I was bringing upon my family and myself. My clients had just as much reason to be discreet as I did. Many of them were married and saw escorts specifically in order to avoid a messy, and expensive, divorce. Even the ones who were single had successful careers and didn't need it known publicly that they had a taste for sex for hire. Most important, we had a special bond that no one else could understand. There was no way any of them would betray me. I was sure of it.

MARK'S OFFER ON THE CONDO at Trump had been accepted, and I was able to move in right away. The address seemed very exclusive to me, and I loved living there from the start. Having a Vegas address was another step toward living my fantasy. I quickly made friends with my neighbors, chatting to whoever crossed my path. I talked a mile a minute, never stopping to think I might be saying the wrong thing or befriending the wrong person.

One night, after seeing a new client, my phone buzzed. It was another of my clients, a regular from San Diego. I smiled, figuring he was sending me a sexy note or letting me know he'd been in town that weekend. And then I read what he'd written: "A man from the Smoking Gun contacted me about a picture of you from your real estate company's website." My hands were shaking as I pushed the button to dial his number.

"What happened?" I said as soon as we got on the phone.

"It was really weird," he said, sounding rattled. "This guy contacted me and introduced himself as a reporter from a website called the Smoking Gun. He asked me if I had ever gone to see an escort named Kelly in Las Vegas, and before I could even try to deny it, he said he'd read my review of you, and so he knew that I had seen you. And then he said he had a photo and he wanted to send it to me and get me to confirm it was the same Kelly I had seen in Vegas. Only when I looked at the woman in the picture, she wasn't named Kelly. She was named Suzy and she was a realtor in Madison, Wisconsin. But the woman in the photo was definitely you."

"What did you say?" I asked, my stomach twisting. I knew members of the Erotic Review were able to exchange messages on the site as a way to share information about girls they liked, and that the Smoking Gun writer could have easily posed as a member in order to infiltrate the escorting world and seek information about me.

"I didn't say anything," he said. "I didn't call him back. I called you instead."

"Thank you," I said, feeling grateful that I had so many amazing, loyal clients. I could still save the day. I knew I could.

"Say it's not me," I said.

"Okay," he said. "I can do that."

I could tell by the tone of his voice that my client found the whole situation very odd. I could also tell that he was nervous that he would be exposed as someone who paid for sex. I quickly tried to reassure him.

"Thank you," I said. "I'm so sorry you had to be bothered with this. It's nothing. Really. Nothing will come of it." To show him I was not the least bit worried, I added, "When will you be in Vegas again?"

After receiving this call, I went back to my regular Vegas routine, without a care in the world. Looking back, of course, this seems impossible to believe. But, as far as I was concerned, I had figured out a way to outsmart this reporter, and that would be the end of it. It never occurred to me that he would contact many more of my clients who had also left reviews for me on the Erotic Review and ask them the same question. It had been easy to dismiss Mark's worry when clients I genuinely liked and trusted had discovered my real identity. This was different, and clearly more serious. But I was more concerned about Mark's reaction to the news than what might actually come of it, and so I put off calling him until the next day.

"Mark, one of my clients called me and told me that a reporter from the website the Smoking Gun had contacted him asking if Kelly, the Vegas escort, was the same person as on our real estate website."

"What do you mean?" Mark said, the panic audible in his voice. "Who was it?"

"Don't worry," I said. "He's a regular from San Diego. I told him to say the woman in the picture wasn't Kelly, and he said he would. We're fine. I'll call Bridget, just in case. It will be okay."

"Bridget can't help us if this reporter really knows who you are and plans to out you. I can't believe I just bought that condo there and it's all falling apart already."

Just the thought of losing the condo, losing my life in Vegas, was enough to make me want to fight back with every ounce of my being.

"I'm not going to let this guy win," I said. "It's all going to be fine. Other people know who I am, and they've never done anything. We don't have anything to worry about."

Mark didn't sound convinced, and neither was I, to be honest. But I certainly wasn't going to stop, or run home. That wasn't even an option. Later in the day, my client called me back to tell me that he'd denied the woman in the photo was Kelly and even said a few things to try to throw this reporter off of my trail. He still sounded a little on edge, and he indicated that he didn't have any plans to come to Vegas for a little while. I told my client that when he did make it back, I would give him a proper thank-you.

Even though I was proud of myself for handling the situation without Mark, it was hard to put the incident out of my mind. For the next week, every time my disposable phone buzzed with an incoming text or call, I steeled myself before answering, worried that it would be another client saying he'd been contacted. I worried that the reporter might be calling me directly. Every time Mark called or e-mailed me, I was afraid it was with the news that the Smoking Gun had done a story on me. In my downtime, I worried about what would happen if my double life were finally exposed. But mostly, I worried about what I would do if I had to stop. That just wasn't an option.

I stayed on the move, always busy, frantic, even. I took as many appointments as I could. I bought myself whatever caught my eye. When all else failed, I did the delicate dance of meeting a man in a bar and convincing him to spend his money on an escort, even though this possibility had been the furthest thing from his mind in the moments just before he met me. As the days passed without any further calls, I put it all out of my mind. As far as I was concerned, I had dodged that bullet, and now it was business as usual.

Chapter 19

WHO I REALLY AM

The service called me and told me that I'd been hired, along with another girl, to go on a golf outing. That sounded like fun, something new. Plus, it involved just the kind of challenge that appealed to my competitive nature.

"Here's the deal," said my contact. "You'll only get paid five hundred dollars to be there all day. I know that's way below your normal daily rate, so just win somebody over, get him to invite you out that night, and you'll make up for it."

The other escort working with me that day was Briana, a wonderful girl I'd worked with before and considered a friend. I also respected the fact that she was supporting her mom and a boyfriend all on her own. We'd been told that the event's organizer hired two girls every year, but the year before the girls were awful and his clients had not been pleased. As Briana and I headed over to the golf course together, we decided that this year was going to be very different.

"This is going to be the best time of their lives," I said.

I was wearing a very short gray sleeveless dress over a sexy lace bra, and nothing else, so I was feeling sexy and free. We worked it from the moment we arrived at the lobby of the golf club. When we saw the guys we'd be escorting, I got very excited. I was immediately drawn to the one who was a dead ringer for Patrick Dempsey. He had such charisma that I wasn't sure if it was the actor or not.

"Holy cow, you look exactly like that actor," I said.

He laughed and pulled up a picture of himself with Patrick Dempsey.

"Are you his stunt double?" I asked.

"No, we just look exactly alike," he said. "I actually met him in person, so we took this picture together."

He might not have been the movie star, but he did look *exactly* like him. I was completely attracted to him, and so I hopped onto his golf cart. One of the other guys was clearly smitten with Briana, so she hopped onto his cart. Our job was to entertain the guys on the golf course, meaning they wanted us to drive the cart around, meet the other guys they were playing with, and flirt with them. I could more than handle that task.

I had my Louis Vuitton bag with me that day, and of course I always carried condoms in this purse, even though I wasn't expecting to need them for an afternoon golf outing. Briana had a purse, too, but apparently she wasn't as prepared as I was. "Do you have any condoms?" she asked me.

"Here," I said, pulling out a strip and handing them to her.

As we drove to the third hole, it was clear the movie star look-alike was very into me, and as I learned more about his fast-paced career in Los Angeles—he actually worked in the movie industry—the feeling was certainly mutual. I was always turned on when I had a client who was particularly successful. The path to the fourth hole led us through a secluded area on the edge of the course, with big mounds of earth that shielded us from view. He drove us around one of the trees to a place where no one could see, and I got out a condom and took care of him right there in the golf cart. It didn't take long, and we were both completely covered again before anyone could see us. I'd never done anything like this, in broad daylight with a client I had only just met. But it also seemed totally normal, and I didn't have a single moment's worry or sense of shame.

Engaging in such risky behavior filled me with adrenaline, and I was as high as I'd ever been. The men couldn't keep their eyes off us, which only encouraged us to take it further. At the next hole, Briana and I both bent over in front of the look-alike so that our skirts lifted just enough to reveal what was underneath and test his concentration. Every hole, it got more extreme. Our clients loved every minute.

On the sixth hole, the look-alike hit the ball into some brush.

"Come and help me find the ball," he said.

The next thing I knew, we were having sex behind a tree. It

wasn't even pleasurable, but I wanted the act itself, the motion and the danger, and even as it was happening, I craved more. As usual, I'd been listening to the same Usher song, "Numb," again and again all morning before I left for the golf course, just like I did every day when I was escorting. The words were stuck in my head: "Let's go numb." By the last hole, Briana and I were both lying on the green with our legs spread, as if they were playing a very adult version of miniature golf and we were one of the obstacles.

From the golf course, we had a thirty-minute drive back to the Strip. While Briana sat texting next to me, I called Mark. In my heightened state, I was swearing like it was nothing and talking freely without any remorse.

"Mark, you're never going to believe the appointment I just had," I said. "We were on a golf outing and my guy, he looked just like Patrick Dempsey, and he liked me right away. Within five minutes, he pulled over behind a tree, and I did the guy right there in the golf cart. And then I did him again in the woods. And the other girl and I, we were out on the green without any underwear, trying to distract the guys while they were playing."

Mark hung up on me, but in my wild mood, this didn't faze me in the least. Just as we had hoped, Briana's guy called her. I was thrilled for her, but hadn't yet heard from the look-alike. And then, my phone buzzed.

I met the look-alike at his room and spent three or four hours with him, earning about two thousand dollars. I was already numb, hardly thinking about what I had to do now when I was with someone. My body just took over.

During a break in the action toward the end of the night, I was lying in bed, naked, drinking a glass of wine, and it all came crashing down on me—everything I had just done with this man, everything I'd done in the past eleven months, what would happen if the Smoking Gun really did expose me. I snapped back into reality, into being Suzy, and I started to cry.

The look-alike was instantly freaked out.

"Hey, hey, it's okay," he said. "What's wrong?"

"You're going to know who I really am soon enough!"

"What do you mean?" he asked, sounding intrigued.

"I can't tell you, but you'll know when it's in the news," I said.

I still wasn't entirely sure why I was crying. I didn't really believe that my story would come out. And while my behavior had gotten more extreme in those late days, I couldn't seem to make myself care about the consequences.

After about five minutes, reality just clicked off, and I was Kelly again. I left soon after that with a promise from him that he'd text me soon.

Not long after that, Mark and Kylie flew into town, and the three of us stayed at our condo at the Trump to spend Thanksgiving together. When they arrived, I was so excited for them to see the condo, my new home. I stood in the lobby with them, facing the bank of elevators.

"Cool," Kylie said. "Our house doesn't have an elevator."

Mark and I laughed.

"You can push the button," he said.

Kylie ran along the row, pushing every up button and craning her neck to watch the windows that showed the elevators' movement between the floors. When we got upstairs, Kylie ran along the corridor, exploring every corner, and once inside, she hurried over to the large wall of windows to look at the view.

"Wow," she said. "You can see everything."

I had found Kylie a place to do gymnastics nearby, and when she went to class there she fell in love right away. By simply calling Bridget, I could get anything I asked for. I used that connection to get tickets to see Shania Twain. Kylie and I walked there, as the concert was in the casino nearby. The next day, I took her to the Fashion Show Mall and bought her whatever she wanted, wanting to make up for the fact that I'd been gone so much. I was showing off for my family, sharing my new life with them. I wanted them to see all that I could give to them now.

Mark's parents came in from Malibu to meet us, and we all had Thanksgiving dinner together at a nice restaurant. I didn't feel the least bit nervous about having my family or my in-laws in town, even though I was very much leading a double life. I was convinced I could get away with anything. By this point, Mark and I had become pretty skilled at acting like everything was fine. I was always happy to see my daughter, and the more time we spent together as a family in Las Vegas, the more I hoped I might make inroads in my plan for us to move there. The mood was strained but not unpleasant. It was the last happy time we'd spend together as a family for a very long time.

During our time in Vegas together, I made my case to him.

"I really think you guys should move here," I said, rushing

to list all of my reasons before he could shut me down. "Kylie's gymnastics here are awesome. She has a great babysitter. She loves the condo and the pool and going to shows. We could get her into private school here, and we'd all be together and have fun, all the time."

"And what about my business?" Mark asked.

"You can quit your job and work out here," I said. "You can work for Trump. They need good real estate brokers like you."

Mark sighed heavily.

"We're not moving to Vegas," he said.

"But Mark . . ."

"You want to move to Vegas, fine, but I want nothing to do with it, and Kylie will not be a part of it."

And that was that.

As much as I wanted to have Mark and Kylie there with me, I really just wanted to never have to go back to Madison again. That was more important to me than my family at that moment, as crazy as it sounds. Even with Mark and Kylie still in Vegas, I went back to what was my normal life now— spray tans, nail salons, dropping thousands of dollars in cash on a pair of boots or a dress, and seeing multiple clients in a day, even picking men up at the bar if the service didn't have enough work for me. I always had to be in motion, which meant I always wanted to be working, and now that I knew the ropes, I made sure I always was.

The organizers of the Rock 'n' Roll Marathon had asked me to make an appearance at their 2012 half marathon, which took place a few days after Thanksgiving, and I was also slated to do television commentary for the race. I really enjoyed my work for this organization, and during the past year I had taken part in several athlete panels, where amateur runners ask their favorite professionals for advice and sometimes autographs. It was a way to give something back to the running community, and I felt honored to speak alongside greats from my sport, like Rod Dixon, Frank Shorter, and Jim Ryun. When I was in the right mind-set, I found the appearances fun and rewarding. But today this was not the case. I was uncomfortable. I was bored. I felt like I was putting on an act. I couldn't wait to be done being Suzy for the day, so I could become Kelly again.

I could be Kelly right now. That's what makes me feel alive, I thought. *Instead, I'm just up here onstage, bragging about myself, repeating the same old shit, over and over.*

I wasn't getting the kind of thrill I craved, even with the stream of fans approaching me to say hello, asking for pictures and autographs. That was nice, but it wasn't what made me feel good. Money, adoration, and sex were what made me feel good. At least the folks at the Rock 'n' Roll Marathon let me run events any way I wanted at that point. The organizers loved my energy and my lack of inhibition. The same was true of the other groups I appeared on behalf of, including Disney and Foot Locker. Instead of giving my usual talk, today I was planning a warm-up for the runners who were there, even though my shimmery short skirt and tiny top weren't exactly athletic wear. I'd given the sound person a CD, and when I heard the opening of my song, I leaped onto the stage. Juiced on the music, and the magic feeling of being in front of a crowd, I worked my body to draw people in, using my physical assets almost like a stripper—a hyperactive stripper, anyway. We had a decent crowd, and all I cared about was that all eyes were on me.

As soon as the music was pumping around me, I felt alive. No more dull conversation, no more expectations of who Suzy was and how she was going to behave. I wanted to have fun and feel good, and so I danced with all I had, even pulling two people from the audience up onto the stage with me. I bounced around in time to the music, shaking my hips and waving my arms over my head, convinced that every man in the crowd was undressing me with his eyes. Scanning the audience as I danced, I saw Mark and Kylie. This was the first Rock 'n' Roll speech they had attended with me, and I decided that Kylie should come up onstage too. So I bounced over to the edge of the platform and pulled her up beside me. Mark wasn't smiling. *He's no fun,* I thought. I didn't need his energy near me, not when the whole city was full of men who wanted to adore me and pay me good money to do so, too. I danced around and around the stage, shaking my hips and waving my arms. Kylie laughed and danced with me, too young to know how sexual my moves were, too naïve to know that the looks people were giving me were disapproving. As soon as the song was done, Mark came up to the side of the stage and gently took Kylie's hand from mine. He then immediately left and took Kylie with him. I was just fine with Mark leaving me alone at the expo center. I was too consumed by mania to see that he was trying to protect Kylie by minimizing her contact with me. When they weren't around, it was easier for me to be Kelly, and that's who I wanted to be.

A group of fans surrounded me once I left the stage, and I laughed and joked with them as we posed for more pictures. I then spotted two of my biggest fans, male groupies who came to every marathon and followed me around. They pushed their way to the front of the crowd. As always, I loved the attention and validation they gave me. They both smiled when they got close, hugging me a little too long. That was fine with me. I liked the feeling of being desired.

"I'm going to head up to my room," I said, glad the Rock 'n' Roll Marathon had gotten me a hotel room for the weekend, because tensions had recently escalated between Mark and me, and I didn't really like to see Mark and Kylie when I was in escorting mode.

"We'll walk you back," said one of my fans.

So there I was, barely dressed in a sparkly purple outfit, with a guy on either side of me, bopping through the convention center and casino. I felt like everyone watched as we walked by, feeding my ever-growing high. The Palazzo hotel was crowded because of the marathon, so we had to push our way through the mob of people. I felt the bodies push against mine, the thrill of the crowd parting ways to let me pass. When we finally reached the narrow hallway that led to the bank of hotel elevators, my phone buzzed with an incoming text. I had a client, and now, the two fans beside me were just a distraction. I quickly said my good-byes, then scrambled to a quiet place to check my message. It was Jim, the client who had previously taken me to an incredible dinner that included a thousand-dollar bottle of wine and had bought me an expensive handbag. Spending more time with this sophisticated, wealthy man was suddenly all I could think about.

I didn't hesitate for an instant, and confirmed the appointment.

Chapter 20

THE SMOKING GUN

I was already thinking about what I was going to wear: yes, it would be my favorite Hervé Léger dress, and always, my five-inch black Christian Louboutin heels. I could practically taste the vodka I would drink and feel the power that Kelly exuded. I waited impatiently for the elevator.

"Suzy," a man's deep voice rose out of the crowd of people behind me.

When I turned and looked at him, I had a weird, out-of-body feeling. This often happened when someone took me out of Kelly mode. I didn't like it.

I figured it had to be another fan, and I had no interest in talking to someone who just wanted an autograph from

Suzy Favor Hamilton. When I looked more closely at the man, something clicked. An uneasy feeling crept into my gut. *Something isn't quite right here,* I thought. Mark had been on high alert for months, trying in vain to get me concerned that I might be exposed. My mania made me feel invincible, so I had simply put Mark's warnings out of my mind. I did the same thing now and smiled at the man, even though I instantly prickled at his cold, judgmental look, the way he loomed over me, as if he'd cornered me.

"My name is William Bastone," he said. "Can I talk to you?"

Oh shit, I thought, instantly frantic. *Mark was right.* I knew that name: it was the man who'd contacted my client, asking about me. Here he was in front of me. Panic set in, twisting my gut. But could this *really* be happening? I was so good at denial, and justifying my actions. Even though I'd recognized his name, and everything about his cocky, self-righteous attitude made me fear what he was going to do next, I was still hoping he'd ask me a couple of questions, which I would deflect, and he'd go on his merry way. I was even annoyed at him for interrupting my ramping excitement about my upcoming client. But as he glowered at me, the truth became obvious. This guy had done his research, and he'd flown out from his office on the East Coast just to come and find me. He knew who I really was. He seemed to feel like he had the right to be cold and disrespectful toward me. It felt like he was judging me from where he stood.

"Can we talk?" he said. "Everything you say to me will be off the record."

"Sure," I said, trying to sound calm. I was actually frazzled, a total mess, but I tried to hold it together. I checked that my phone was still in my purse, the mania dropping away with every second. "Can we step out into the casino to talk?" I asked.

Bastone nodded, and I walked away from the elevators to the edge of the casino floor. With him following close behind me, I focused on the story I had prepared in case this moment ever happened. Once we were away from the crowd, I was tempted to run, but I stayed put and concentrated on doing the best acting job ever. *Can I talk my way out of this? Maybe.* That was Kelly thinking, confident and in control. *I'm Kelly now,* I reminded myself, *and he can't ruin my life.* I felt a tiny glimmer of hope. Everyone else in my life had disappeared. But I would fight for Kelly, even if that meant denying her existence.

"We know who you are," Bastone said, his voice firm, uncaring, his face devoid of any emotion. "We know you're Kelly. We know what you're doing."

He quickly presented his evidence to me.

"We've matched the dates you made appearances for the Rock 'n' Roll Marathon, here in Vegas and in other cities, with the dates the service posted that Kelly was in those cities," he said.

I'd never actually seen clients in any of the cities he mentioned, but when the service had asked if they could do this to attract more business for me, I'd agreed, without ever considering that there might be ramifications later. "We were anonymously contacted by a gentleman who indicated that you were Kelly," he continued. "We have photos of you as Kelly. And I've contacted multiple clients of yours, who, when shown photos of you in your regular, daily life, confirmed that you were the Kelly they'd slept with."

Holy shit, what is happening to me right now? I thought. *I have to stay calm.* But for the first time in the year I'd been working as an escort in Vegas, the facts of what I'd done hit me. I knew my life was ruined, over. My heart plummeted. "That's absolutely ridiculous," I said in my most matter-of-fact tone, trying desperately to act cool. "You're wrong. You have no idea what's going on."

I made myself look him straight in the eye. Mark's anxiety about the situation had inspired me to work out a plan, in the quiet hours of the night when I allowed myself to think about it. "I'm having an affair, and this man who told you I'm Kelly is lying," I said. "He's upset I won't marry him, and he's trying to get revenge."

With the evidence he'd just provided me, I knew my story would fall on deaf ears, and yet I had to at least try.

"No, I don't buy that one bit," he said. "You're lying. And I know you're lying. I've seen the website. I've talked with your clients. It's you."

I was used to guys fawning all over me, and praising me, and being so nice to me, buying me drinks and expensive jewelry, telling me how gorgeous I was and how I was the sexiest, most interesting woman they'd ever met, how they wished their wives were like me, how they wished I *was* their wife. And now, I could feel this man demeaning me. I could feel him talking to me like I was dirt. He had his story, and he looked so proud of himself. I didn't want to be near him another minute, but I knew I had to do something, and fast. "Listen, why don't we go up to my room, and we can talk about this more?"

"Absolutely not," he shot back, stepping away from me. "There's no way I'm going to your room with you."

He glared at me, and I realized he probably thought I was going to try to lure him up there to have sex with him. It hadn't actually occurred to me to try to seduce him, even though that's how I usually got my way these days. I just wanted to talk to him and convince him to see things from my point of view. "We need to meet and talk somewhere other than your room," he said.

"Well, I have to go somewhere right now," I said.

"I'm flying back to NYC tomorrow afternoon, so let's meet tomorrow morning," he said. "I need a statement from you. It can soften the blow for you of the article I write."

What is he talking about? He's going to ruin my life and my family, no matter what I do or say! I was so sickened at this moment, but I nodded. We set a time and place to meet, and I walked away.

When I got up to my room, I slowly opened the door, wanting to delay the moment when I had to tell Mark for as long as possible. I picked up my phone. I didn't want to call my husband, but I knew I had no choice. I was trembling as I listened to the phone ring. As soon as Mark answered, a rush of panicked words escaped from my mouth. I wasn't able to speak clearly, but after several false starts, I finally managed a complete sentence.

"It was just like you said it would be," I said. "He found me. Please come over here as quickly as you can."

The tears started rolling down my cheeks. As we talked, I looked in the bathroom mirror, not quite sure who I saw staring back at me. I'd been angry at Mark for trying to talk sense, but I needed his help desperately now. Since we'd started dating when I was eighteen, he'd always been my rock, my confidant, and my sounding board. And even though shaking off what had begun to feel like his controlling influence had been part of why I had taken this path, now I would do whatever he told me. It felt like too little, far too late.

Would Mark leave me and take my daughter away from me? How would I tell my parents, my siblings, my in-laws? Would they all disown me? They would never understand this world and what it had come to mean to me. They would never understand how I had become stronger, more powerful as Kelly. With the phone still in my hand, I fell to the cold floor and curled up in a ball, crying. *Help me*, I thought. *Help me, please.*

After a while, I got up and paced the room until Mark finally knocked on the door. When he walked in, I could read his thoughts in his body language: *I told you so.* I couldn't stand it.

"Don't look at me like that!" I screamed at him.

I hated the idea of yelling in front of Kylie, who had come in with Mark, but I was beyond caring now.

"Calm down," he said. "What did this man say?"

I presented the evidence just as Bastone had laid it out for me.

"Well, he is going to destroy you," Mark said. This was

not what I wanted to hear. I needed Mark to rescue me, and he saw the situation as hopeless. I hated him right now. He couldn't save me. Worse, he didn't *want* to. In my head, I just kept hearing his voice saying, again and again, "I told you so. I told you so." I felt there had to be a way out, somehow, and I paced the room, frantically trying to work out a solution.

"Can you please try to calm down?" Mark said.

I didn't even look up at him, just kept pacing.

"Can you *please* try to calm down, Suzy?" he repeated.

His words only made me more upset.

"How can I calm down?" I said. "My life is over."

"Well, what the fuck did you expect?" he said.

Mark held out his hand for Kylie and led her toward the door. I knew that I was on the verge of a complete and total breakdown. "Where are you going?" I screamed, panicked at the thought of being left alone.

"I'm taking Kylie back to the condo," he said. "She doesn't need to see you like this."

He leaned down to Kylie, amazingly skilled at keeping his cool.

"Say good night to your mom," he said.

"Good night, Mommy," she said.

Looking at her sweet face, knowing what was coming, was almost enough to break my heart. Almost. When the door shut behind them, I looked around the empty hotel room, knowing there was no way I was going to be able to sleep that night. I knew there was also no way I was going to be able to hold it together during an appointment with Jim, the client I was supposed to see, so I texted him to cancel.

Mark later told me that when he walked Kylie back to the Trump that night, he tried to explain what she'd just seen: "Mommy's brain doesn't always work right. That's not your mommy, and you know that." Apparently, Kylie understood as much as any little girl could. Alone in my hotel room, I finally stretched out on the bed, but my mind's racing kept me awake. There was no way I could lose the best part of my life and return to my normal existence in Madison. And what would be left of that reality anyway? I would lose my family, my child. I thought it would be better to die. Somehow, I gathered the strength to get ready for my meeting the next morning. At nine, I walked up to the Starbucks where we'd agreed to meet. William Bastone was already there, sitting at a table outside, looking just as pleased with himself, and as disgusted with me, as he had the day before.

I walked right by him, trying not to show my devastation and desperation.

"I'm just going to get some tea," I said.

When I had my cup of tea in hand, I sat down next to him on a bench outside, the knot in my stomach tightening.

"Listen, everything you say to me is off the record," he said. "But I'm writing the story, whether you like it or not."

Mark had gone into fix-it mode right away. He immediately had the service take down my web page and removed all pictures of me from our real estate website. He also got rid of every picture he could find of me online, especially those where I was with Kylie. Our main concern was Kylie and how we could protect her from what was about to happen, and so we did everything we could to keep her life as normal as possible. Mark had a manager he trusted at the real estate firm, and he called him and told him as much as he felt he could. When the news broke, it would definitely not go unnoticed among our managers and peers, so Mark wanted to prepare them for what was coming without being too specific about the details.

"Suzy is resigning. Something has happened. And this will be best for everybody."

In a show of solidarity, the manager told him I could continue working with the agency on a limited basis, but Mark knew that would never work.

"Trust me," he said. "She's going to have to resign."

Chapter 21

EXPOSURE

Mark and I eventually became fairly certain we knew who had tipped off the Smoking Gun: a regular who'd become angry with me when I'd canceled several appointments with him, his disappointment and hurt feelings turning to a desire for revenge. While there was some satisfaction in knowing the truth, it didn't change the fact that I was going to be publicly outed, or that we wouldn't know when it was happening until the article was published. Mark had already taken all the steps he could think of to minimize the impact on our daughter and on our business. But we still had to face one of the hardest experiences of all. Mark called his dad.

"We have to tell you something," Mark said, his voice trembling. "I need you to support Suzy, regardless of what I'm going to say to you."

Even as Mark explained as much as he knew and made it clear that this was no practical joke, they couldn't believe what we were telling them. As it began to sink in, they were consumed by shock and anger.

"What the hell was she thinking?" Mark's dad asked. "How could this possibly happen?"

"I know," Mark said, tears in his eyes. "We're so, so sorry. I thought it might never come out, so I was covering and hoping for the best, but I'm convinced it's going to happen soon."

My parents took it much harder. They lived in a small town, where everybody knew everybody's business as it was, and they would never be able to escape the humiliation I caused them, which is something I regret to this day. Plus, they still lived in Wisconsin, where I was well known, and they were very aware how much this story would impact the area. It would be front-page news. And they were as concerned about their image, and our family's image, as they'd always been. Plus, in many ways, I was still their perfect little girl.

"That is not you," my dad said.

"I know, Dad," I said. "I'm sorry."

"We're going to bed soon," he said. "I'll tell your mom in the morning. I don't want her worrying about this tonight. Where are you? Are you safe? Is Mark with you?"

"Yes, Dad," I said.

Still certain he knew what was best for me, he told me in no uncertain terms that I should dye my hair, change my name, take Kylie out of school, and move to another country. Without responding, I hung up the phone, realizing that they weren't going to be any help at all. All of this was going to be hard enough on Kylie as it was, and Mark and I didn't want to uproot her life on top of everything else. Mark wanted to try to keep things as normal as possible for her. I could see him really stepping up, and I was so grateful to him for it.

Two weeks later, on December 20, we were staying at the guesthouse at Mark's parents' house, getting ready for Christmas. I woke up early and did my normal morning routine, going for a run down the hill from their house and along the Pacific Coast Highway to the Starbucks where I liked to get a cup of tea and a blueberry scone. I was standing in line to place my order when my phone started buzzing. It was Mark. "You'd better get home right now," he said.

"Why?" I asked, still lingering in the innocent place.

"The story just broke," he said.

As we were talking, the man in front of me looked up from his smartphone, then down at whatever he was reading, and then up at me again, with an amused expression on his face.

I turned and walked out without getting anything and ran the three miles back to my in-laws' house as quickly as I could. I was completely numb for the rest of the day, barely aware of what was happening on the periphery of my attention, where Mark was doing his best to sort through the hundreds of e-mails that were pouring into our joint account, including interview requests from everyone from CNN to Dr. Phil and a meeting opportunity with the porn company Vivid, as well as an incredible amount of hate mail, deleting the most

hurtful notes before I could read them. He didn't always succeed, though, and I stumbled upon messages that said I was
a slut and whore, that I was going to hell, that I should kill
myself like my brother had. Meanwhile, in the main house, my
mother-in-law obsessively watched hours of coverage on Fox
and CNN, where topless images of me in sexy poses were being
shown again and again and again. I remained bizarrely calm.

When I woke up the next morning, the calm was gone.
The darkest thoughts possible ran through my mind on a
continual loop: I was a whore. I had shamed my parents, my
husband, our family, my entire state. It would be better for
everyone if I were dead. I didn't say any of this out loud to
Mark, but I think he could tell. I kept sneaking off to read the
nasty e-mails on my phone. Finally, he came up behind me,
smiling as well as he could.

"Hiking?" he said. "I think we need to get out."

Leaving Kylie with his parents, we climbed into the car and
drove down the hill toward our usual hiking spot, twenty-
five miles away, at Sycamore Canyon. It was another perfect
Southern California day, the sunshine glinting off the blue
waves of the Pacific Ocean, but none of it could reach me or
lighten my mood. Mark said something that set me off, and
I went ballistic. My hypersensitivity was at an all-time high.
My entire world was caving in. I wanted someone to blame.
As far as I was concerned, he was the real problem. He was
trying to control me and force me to stop escorting, which I
didn't want to do. He had driven me to this point, and I hated
him. As we screamed at each other for the next fifteen minutes, he turned the car around, since hiking was clearly out

of the question. I wanted to get away from him, and I pulled myself farther and farther away, toward the other side of the car, but I couldn't put enough distance between us. I wanted this nightmare to end. I wanted to stop everything. I choked on the tears pouring down my face, great sobs shaking my body, nothing inside me but pain. My mind was spinning with a single thought: *end it all, end it all, end it all.*

A vision came into my mind: I saw myself opening the car door and hitting the asphalt as the car behind us slammed into my body, flipping me over and over, my arms and legs flailing. It could all be over in a second. All I had to do was release the door handle and just fall out. *Please let me die.* I leaned away even farther from Mark, pressing my head against the window, and reached for the handle. I could no longer hear the sound of Mark's voice. I just wanted out. Mark turned to look at me and, seeing what I was doing, slammed the brakes. I flew into the dashboard, the force of the impact bringing me back to the present moment.

"What the fuck?" he yelled.

All I could do was let my head fall into my hands and keep crying. Mark pulled the car over onto the side of the road.

"Should I take you to the hospital?" he said, sounding dazed and confused. "Where do I take you?"

In January, I was finally diagnosed with bipolar disorder.

Epilogue
A WORK IN PROGRESS

I t is a crisp, fall morning. I dropped Kylie off at school about an hour ago, and now I'm ready for my time. I look forward to this time, when I can move in the way my body knows best, wind in my hair, finding the rhythm that feels as natural as breathing.

I run now for the freedom it gives me. I run because it feels good. I run because it is good for me—for my heart and for my head. But it isn't all I do. I am still constantly in motion; in my running shoes, on my bike, on my yoga mat, exercise is my drug of choice now.

In these moments, on the path with my feet hitting the ground, I feel peaceful. I am myself, living the life I want,

not the one that others expect from me or the one that I created out of fantasy and confusion. My life now isn't perfect.
Far from it. But it is a life of contentment, and for this I am
incredibly grateful.

I am grateful for the little moments in life, like walking my
daughter to school, sharing a meal together as a family, dancing
to our favorite songs in the kitchen while we bake chocolate
chip cookies. I am grateful that the love of my life stood by
me through the destruction that was my illness. If I'm honest,
I wonder if maybe he cared about me more than I cared about
myself. I almost destroyed our family, and myself, but Mark
stayed, finding the strength to do so once I received my bipolar
diagnosis, and he dedicated himself to learning as much as he
could about my illness and supporting me to get better. And
when the time came to start again, he was the one who told
me that I had to forgive myself first before I could move on.
Without him, I never would have found that courage. Without
his love, I might never have been diagnosed. I might still be
stuck in my cycle of risky behavior, always pushing for more,
more, more. I might even have pushed too far. Bipolar disorder
needs an outlet. Sex, drugs, alcohol, danger, adrenaline—these
all feed the mania that sets a bipolar brain on fire.

Being diagnosed wasn't enough to turn off my mania. The
year that followed my diagnosis was actually the most challenging of all, for my family and for me. Even when I was
prescribed Lamictal, the drug that finally quieted my mind,
it took months for us to find the right dosage. Until then, I
self-medicated with alcohol and Xanax and when nothing else
gave me the sensation I craved, I occasionally slipped up and

resorted to my previous coping mechanisms. Finally, with the help of a skilled mental health team, we identified the triggers that were setting me off: my job, my family, and certain aspects of my marriage. We cleaned up the wreckage I had created, paying the taxes I owed for my escorting and finally making it clear to all of my clients that my time as an escort was over forever. We made a plan to manage my exposure to my triggers, so I would be set off as little as possible. And we found better ways for me to achieve the high I craved, including intense exercise and travel, often paired together, such as a challenging hike in a beautiful new locale.

With Mark's support, I stopped feeding the flames, and I reached deep down into my soul to find the true source of my pain and to begin to heal it. With Mark's example of unconditional love as their guide, Mark's parents also stood by me with so much love and support, as did most of my family, many of our friends, a good amount of people in Madison, as well as some in the international mental health and running communities. I know it wasn't easy for my parents to come to terms with what I'd done. At first, they focused on the way my illness had manifested itself, instead of my illness. But, recently, they have begun to understand more and offer their encouragement, which means so much to me. When I consider the wealth of love and support in my life, I feel so very fortunate and grateful.

It is not easy to admit you have a problem, that you are sick. Denial grabs hold and clings for dear life. Denial can ruin lives as much as mental illness can. I know that now. The denial in my own family, the way we looked away from the very truth before us, was destructive. My parents can't be blamed for what happened to Dan, or to me, of course. They did the best they could. We all did. Our mental illness was up to the algebra of genetics, our unlucky equation. But treatment was and is available. So many people are left untreated, even today when there is much aid available to them. You don't have to hide or be ashamed for being sick now. You can reach out and be helped, and thank God for that.

As I run, I feel my muscles loosen, stretching and contracting from memory. It was once my running that made me a role model, even though I had little desire for the attention or that burden. I came to hate the thing I loved most, the thing I was born to do. But now, I have a new purpose, new goals that have nothing to do with crossing the finish line first. I want to share my story. I want to have courage and keep fighting. I want to show the world, but mostly my daughter, that you have to live your life for yourself, and that with love and help you can claw your way back from a dark place. I hope my daughter never goes toward darkness, but if she does I'll be there to tell her that shame and guilt are wasted emotions. The shame and guilt that I wrestled with kept me stuck for a long time. And while I am deeply sorry for the hurt I caused my family, I know that I didn't do it out of malice or lack of care. I had no other choice but to act as I did. That is the power of bipolar disorder.

No one asks for mental illness, but now I see my long battle as a gift. I would never have gone down this road if I weren't bipolar, but if I weren't bipolar I wouldn't have found my voice to live my truth and tell my story, and I wouldn't be here now to help others to know that they are not alone.

ACKNOWLEDGMENTS

My incredibly compassionate daughter, Kylie, who gave me the strength to get well with her openness and ability to understand mental illness with such a loving heart.

Mark, the most amazing man I know, for not giving up on me, and reminding me that shame is a waste of time and energy.

My parents, who didn't always fully understand me but always loved me. I love you dearly.

My in-laws, Darrell and Sandy, for being there when I needed you most.

Everyone at Dey Street and HarperCollins, for your belief in my story.

Carrie Thornton, for her support, and for always telling me that my book can help so many people.

My agents, Nena and Jan, for reaching out to me, and for displaying such great patience, something I am so grateful to have learned through this process.

Sarah Tomlinson, for her patience with a bipolar girl trying to tell her story. Thanks for being a huge part of my journey toward recovery. I am very lucky to have you in my life.

Dr. Aurelia Nattiv, my doctor at UCLA, who was there for me in my darkest time and has been a dear friend.

Dr. Dan Begel, my psychiatrist in Santa Monica, who diagnosed me and helped to find the right medication for me.

Dr. Claudia Reardon, my psychiatrist in Madison, for your exceptional care.

Dr. Erri Hewitt, my psychologist in Madison, for helping me to understand myself, and putting the pieces of the puzzle together, which empowered me in a way I didn't think possible.

My brother Dan, for being such a kind-hearted and compassionate person. I wish I'd had the same understanding of bipolar disorder when I was young that I do now. Your memory lives on in a powerful way that will help so many others.

Mary, who had such a huge impact on my life. I am so blessed to have had you as my friend.

The friends, and even strangers, who offered me their support and did not judge me without knowing my story.

ABOUT THE AUTHOR

Suzy Favor Hamilton is a three-time Olympian for women's middle distance running. She is a sought-after public speaker—addressing eating disorders, mental illness, and the struggles that young athletes face—as well as a yoga instructor. Favor Hamilton lives in California.